ANA NO

Goodnight Lisa

See You In The Morning

A MOTHER'S FIGHT
FOR HER DISABLED CHILD

Sarah
GRACE
PUBLISHING
Dyslexic Friendly

First published 2019 by Sarah Grace Publishing
an imprint of Malcolm Down Publishing Ltd.
www.malcolmdown.co.uk

British Library Cataloguing in Publication Data
A catalogue record for this book is available from the British Library.

ISBN 978-1-912863-37-2

Cover design by Esther Kotecha
Art direction by Sarah Grace

Printed in the UK

Some names have been changed to protect identities

Contents

Prologue

Lisa was born to be famous. Within hours of her birth, news of the 'punk rock baby' spread through the hospital's maternity wing. Paparazzi took photos of the newborn baby with hair like a toilet brush. I wondered if my daughter's black spiky hair had anything to do with the copious amounts of chocolate gateaux I'd consumed while pregnant. A healthy diet of fresh fruit and vegetables had not been completely forsaken, of course, but who was I to deny the sweet cravings? Girls are born with a chocolate gene and mine had gone into overdrive.

Prior to my bump days I had weighed a very respectable nine stone. Over the following forty weeks, I managed to gain a few more, and eventually tipped the scales at a voluptuous twelve stone. My belly was so large that I had problems finding a maternity dress that would circumnavigate my girth. In a moment of desperation, I imagined phoning a marquee company to enquire if they made tents in my size. The hospital's radiographer assured me there was only *one* baby in there. My feet and ankles had become so swollen that I couldn't get my shoes on and had to borrow my husband's size eleven moccasins. All in all, I looked as glamorous as a ballet-dancing hippopotamus.

On reaching my due date, I was admitted on the antenatal ward because of high blood pressure. When the nurse checked my blood pressure, she raised one eyebrow and repeated the procedure.

'That can't be right, it must be broken,' she muttered, and went to fetch another sphygmomanometer.

After her third attempt, a doctor was summoned. My blood pressure was dangerously high and I was given an injection, after which it soared even higher!

That evening, halfway through visiting time, I was chatting with my husband, Jonathan, when I felt a popping sensation in my nether regions, followed by a gush of fluid. I pressed the call button. The nurse seemed miffed that her tea break had been interrupted. I was tempted to apologise and ask for a cork so she could finish her cup of Earl Grey. It became apparent why my belly had been so huge by the copious amounts of amniotic fluid which saturated the bed. The nurse announced that it was time to go to the labour ward. There was no sign of the flow abating. I half-expected her to fetch a canoe!

Each contraction was accompanied by the most awful back pain because my baby was lying head down with her back against mine. This confirmed my suspicions that my baby had not read any good books about birthing before making her grand entrance into the world. In an attempt to speed up my labour, I was given various drugs intravenously. Startled by the intensity of the contractions, I swore to myself, *never again*! Thankfully, the midwife knew how and where to rub my back to help alleviate the pain while Jonathan stood at a safe distance looking completely nonplussed.

Twenty hours and three doses of the analgesia pethidine later, a midwife broke the harrowing news.

'You're one-and-a-half centimetres dilated.'

I could not believe my ears! After a long and sleepless night, it was too much to bear and all I wanted was to get the baby *out*! I felt a strong urge to escape through the window and go home. Consumed with exhaustion and despair, I lay back on the bed and gave up. Jonathan, also tired from spending the night at my bedside, went off to the toilet and had a good cry. My contractions ground to a halt and I was labelled 'Failure to Progress'.

All of a sudden, the foetal heart monitor sounded an alarm, the door was flung open and midwives filled the room. My baby was in severe foetal distress and I was rushed to theatre for an emergency Caesarean section. There was no time for an epidural and Jonathan was not allowed to be present. The anaesthetist handed me an oxygen mask and I took a few deep breaths, but removing the mask to breathe some normal air, received a stern reprimand from the anaesthetist.

'Now we've got to start all over again!'

Grabbing the mask, he held it firmly in place while I lay on the operating table feeling acutely upset at being told off, and afraid of what I might find when I woke up. *If* I woke up. A shooshing sound filled my ears as I slowly descended into darkness. It was not a pleasant experience.

When I woke up, all I could feel was a searing pain like a red-hot poker across my lower abdomen. A nurse standing beside the trolley leaned forward.

'Congratulations, you have a beautiful baby girl. Would you like to see her?'

I could only concentrate on the pain and snapped, 'No!'

My experience of labour had been so traumatic that I wanted absolutely nothing to do with my baby. Within minutes of being transferred to a side room in the post-natal ward, I was fast asleep, and for the next fourteen hours remained completely oblivious to the world.

Less than a year previously, I had worked on the same ward as an auxiliary nurse and loved the job, especially sitting with the mums while they talked about their experience on the labour ward, and looking after the newborn babies at night while their mothers slept. Now I was on the receiving end, waking up in familiar surroundings and being cared for by staff I had worked alongside.

Wracked with guilt for rejecting my baby, I was now desperate to see her. Then came a sound I knew only too well – the squeaking of cot wheels and the cries of hungry babies as nurses transported the infants from nursery to ward. A mild sense of panic began to set in.

Where's my baby?

Why isn't she here?

Is she in Special Care?

Are they keeping her from me because I didn't want to see her?

After what seemed like an eternity, the door opened and a nurse peeked in.

'Oh good, you're awake,' she said softly. 'There's someone here to see you.' She promptly disappeared around the corner. A few minutes later she returned, pushing a cot.

The moment I set eyes on my daughter I fell in love with her. She was so beautiful and, oh my goodness, what a lot of hair! Weighing a healthy eight pounds, she seemed perfect in every way. Taking a deep breath, her little face turned bright red and she bellowed the unmistakable cry of 'Feed me; feed me *now!*'

I held my daughter to my breast and she took her fill of mother's finest. After a few successful burps she settled down, content. Slowly bending my legs at the knee, wincing from the stitches, I laid my daughter on her back against the blanket and we spent the next few moments gazing at each other.

'Hello, Lisa,' I whispered.

As I unfolded her warm flannelette wrap, I was pleased to see that my baby appeared pink and healthy. Her little arms reached out and tiny fingers grasped mine. Released from their cocoon, her legs began to kick. Everything seemed perfectly normal.

At just one-day-old, my baby girl had taken up permanent residence in my heart. From that day on, everything which affected my child would affect me. As I gazed into my daughter's eyes the atmosphere in the room became still, permeated with a silence that was almost tangible.

But in that moment, from somewhere deep inside of me, I also knew there was something wrong.

CHAPTER ONE

Meeting Jonathan

A chance encounter in a sleepy English village held the key to a future way beyond anything I could possibly have imagined. A naïve sixteen-year-old on holiday with her parents, I was blissfully unaware that the stage had been set. The interior of the caravan park clubhouse certainly offered no hint that destiny beckoned, decorated as it was in typical 1970s British pub fashion with beige-painted walls, exposed oak beams, plain wooden tables and chairs, a lone dartboard surrounded by tiny holes in the wall and, of course, the obligatory pool table. I rarely frequented pubs, preferring to remain at home with a good book, or delve into a stack of encyclopaedia magazines to quench my thirst for knowledge.

My father returned from the bar, drinks in hand – a pint of lager, a shandy for Mother, and an orange juice for me – and joined us at the table. My father could spot a wolf in sheep's clothing a mile away. Born and raised in a remote farmhouse on a Croatian mountainside, he kept a close eye on his family and was fiercely protective of his youngest daughter.

The clubhouse pulsated with the chatter of locals and tourists. Swirling patterns of cigarette smoke wafted through the air, an inconsequential vapour drifting through time and space. I glanced into the dregs of my juice and sighed.

And then I saw him.

'Tall, dark and handsome' doesn't even begin to describe him as he stood behind the bar serving drinks. His olive complexion, smouldering brown eyes and shoulder-length mane of black wavy hair was irresistible. Just one glance at his tall, muscular physique, accentuated by a white cheesecloth shirt and dark-blue jeans was enough to raise my temperature. My defences melted like ice cream on a barbecue.

When my parents announced they were tired and returned to their caravan, I decided to stay a while and have another drink. Forty minutes later I was about to leave when the handsome barman sauntered in my direction, heading straight for me. Frozen to the spot, my internal organs felt like they were performing cartwheels and backflips. When Mr Muscle reached my table, he leaned towards me and with confident charm, plus a scent of 'come hither' aftershave, said, 'Hi, I haven't seen you here before. Are you staying on-site?'

Somehow, I managed to respond, 'Yes, I'm here with my parents.'

Leaning closer still, the tall, dark stranger introduced himself. 'Pleased to meet you, I'm Jonathan. Can I walk you back to your caravan?'

The broad Dorset accent was a dead giveaway. He wasn't Italian after all, but it made no difference.

All I could manage was: 'OK.'

Jonathan and I walked into the cool night air, chatting along the way. Employed full-time as a radio technician for the Ministry of Defence, he only worked at the clubhouse now and then to help out when they were short-staffed. Aged nineteen, Jonathan lived nearby with his parents, an Irish father and Welsh mother. The perfect gentleman, I felt safe in his company. I informed Jonathan that I had recently completed a pre-nursing course at college, although at the time I had no intention of pursuing a career in nursing.

Jonathan and I walked along the track leading to the caravan, a faint light glowing within. Standing over six-feet tall to my five-feet-four, I was in no doubt that should I ever need a bodyguard, I was in good company. He didn't seem to mind that I was quiet and reserved; maybe I posed a challenge to him. On reaching the door, Jonathan paused. There was no doubt about it, I was a moth to his light bulb. Holding my breath and wondering what was going to happen next, Jonathan had his next move carefully orchestrated.

'Can I see you again?'

'Yes,' I said, my mind racing with *are you going to kiss me or not?* He didn't.

Flashing a broad smile with a brilliant set of pearly whites, my escort turned around and strode into the night. Snuggled in my sleeping bag, I lay awake for hours, reliving the scene over and over again in my mind.

The next morning, I was abruptly awakened by my mother announcing, 'Quick, get up! Jonathan's here!' I scrambled out of bed so fast that I crashed onto the floor in a dishevelled heap. Regaining my composure, I dashed to the mirror. It was not a pretty sight. My face resembled a wrinkled mushroom and my 'bed hair' looked as if I'd slept in a thunderstorm. It was enough to make a grown man faint.

I darted into the tiny bathroom cubicle to make myself appear less scary as Jonathan knocked on the caravan door. My mother could have been nominated for an Oscar, responding calmly, 'She'll be out in a minute,' as if we had all been up since the crack of dawn. With all the nonchalance I could muster, I glided past her, pretending not to hear her remonstration of: 'What about your breakfast?' I left the confines of the caravan and stepped into my future.

Jonathan's family lived in a terraced cottage down a quiet country lane in Dorset. His mother cast a quizzical eye over me. Devout Roman Catholics, she asked if I went to church.

'No, I don't,' I replied, adding, 'I did go to Sunday school as a child, though,' so as not to appear a complete heathen.

The scene beyond the back garden was beautiful, a small wooden gate leading straight into a forest. Jonathan informed me that when he was a baby, his mother put him in his pram outside, come rain or shine, because 'fresh air was good for you'. It seemed to pay off because he rarely caught a cold, in spite of the fact that he wore jeans and a T-shirt throughout winter.

My holiday in Dorset was over too quickly and it was soon time to return home. Jonathan and I kept in touch on a regular basis by phone or letter, and every now and then took the train to our respective parents' homes to spend the weekend.

When I was eighteen my parents announced they were getting a divorce, which shook me to the core. My father packed his bags and moved out, my sister left home to share a flat with a friend, my brother painted his entire bedroom black and my mother had a nervous breakdown.

A few months later, Jonathan proposed and I said yes.

CHAPTER TWO

A Glimpse into the Future

There's nothing like being thrown in at the deep end. My knowledge of any form of disability, whether physical or learning impairment, was almost nonexistent. I had never had a conversation with a person in a wheelchair before and I had never met anyone with a learning difficulty. Any preconceived notions about disability were about to be challenged and irrevocably changed.

Situated near the end of my road was a school for children with special needs. I had walked past this school many times on my way to the bus stop and, to be honest, hadn't given it much thought. Disabled people made me feel uneasy, especially if they shouted incomprehensibly in the middle of a store, or if their bodies jerked in an uncontrollable manner. It's easy to judge what you don't understand.

At the age of seventeen, the pre-nursing course placement for my work experience just happened to be in this very school. On the morning of my first day, I was nervous and had no idea what to expect. Walking through the main gates and into the school, my first impression of the reception area was favourable, the environment colourful and welcoming. On the far side of the entrance hall was a bright-blue wheelchair. I didn't even know wheelchairs came in different colours. A large wooden seat with a table attached, similar to a high chair but for an older child, was placed in one corner. On the walls, a gallery of photos displayed children engaged in classroom activities and outdoor pursuits and alongside those were photographs of staff with their names below.

Just as I began to wonder what to do next, a man wearing a suit approached me, extended his hand and gave me a firm but friendly handshake.

'Don't look so worried!' he said, smiling.

The headteacher's welcoming manner put me at ease straightaway. Mr Robertson led me into his office and offered a brief summary about the school. He told me the pupils, aged eleven to nineteen, had a range of severe learning difficulties, sensory or physical impairments, and behavioural problems. Every class teacher was assisted by at least one teaching assistant to help with the children's personal needs, which included toileting and changing nappies.

The school buses were due to arrive at any moment and it was 'all hands on deck'. Mr Robertson and I stood at the ready, although I didn't have a clue what to do. Minutes later, I was assigned the role of guard duty and instructed to stand inside the front door to prevent any children from escaping. I wondered what on earth I was supposed to do if a child did try to escape!

A steady stream of bright yellow buses flowed through the gates and drew to a halt on the forecourt, a few feet from the main entrance. Immediately a team of staff members and volunteers appeared in reception, wearing the same polo shirts bearing the school logo, and flowed en masse through the doors to help children disembark from the buses. Bearing in mind I had rarely seen a disabled child before, I was taken aback by the endless flow of them.

Each bus had a driver, plus one escort.

'Jodie's thrown up again,' said an escort to a volunteer.

'Christopher's wet his pants, he'll need changing!' said another.

Adults and children mingled together amidst a varied assortment of wheelchairs and walking frames, schoolbags and backpacks. Some of the children ambled into the school with an unusual gait pattern, others wore protective headgear. One teenager made a loud moaning sound and another shrieked. A few dribbled incessantly. One of the younger children tried to make a run for it, broke free from the group and headed straight for the main gates, which were still open. A member of staff spotted him and immediately gave chase, catching the boy and coaxing him back towards the school. The staff were skilled and moved like clockwork. Mindful of possible escapees, I secretly hoped and prayed that I wouldn't have to try to stop anyone from running away. Little did I know that I was about to be taught a lesson I would never forget.

Just inside the main doors, a teenage boy and girl with Down's syndrome sat side by side engaged in conversation. The boy looked up at me and with a gleam in his eye proudly announced, 'We're getting married, we are!' They were clearly smitten with each other. Could two people with Down's syndrome get married and live together? I had absolutely no idea. I didn't know how to respond.

Suddenly the lovelorn boy stood to his feet and without a word strode towards the open door. My mind raced with the instruction, 'Don't let them escape.' I sprang into action and leapt to the door and in one giant step, blocked the teenager's exit.

'I don't think you're allowed to go out there,' I said, with as much authority as I could muster.

'Do you mind, I'm going to ask Mr Brown if he would like a cup of tea!' responded the lad, glaring indignantly.

Rendered speechless, I stood rooted to the spot while the confident young lad strode past me and out of the door. Mr Brown (the bus driver) had completed his morning rounds and the teenager was simply attending to his daily task of providing him with a cup of tea, to which he responded, 'Yes, I'd love a cuppa. Thank you, Stephen.'

Prior to this encounter with Stephen, my opinion about disabled people was based on how I felt and not on the facts. I had been given a glimpse into a world that I knew so little about.

But I would know soon.

CHAPTER THREE

Looking for Answers

After trying for over two years to conceive, my husband and I were delighted when I became pregnant. The following nine months passed without incident, apart from the high blood pressure and swollen ankles a couple of weeks before my due date. Employed as a telecommunications engineer, Jonathan brought in a decent wage, which meant that I could be a stay-at-home mum.

By the age of four months, our daughter, Lisa, was already sleeping through the night. Sometimes I woke up in the morning with a start, realising that she had gone all night without a feed and, rushing to her bedroom, would discover Lisa gazing happily at the colourful mobile above her cot. She always greeted me with a smile.

We enjoyed family outings together, especially the park; feeding the ducks was a favourite pastime of Lisa's. Jonathan spent most Saturdays playing rugby, and if the weather was nice, Lisa and I would visit in the afternoons to watch the game.

For the first eleven months, our daughter seemed to be developing normally. Routine tests performed at our local health clinic indicated that her vision and hearing were both normal. The physical milestones of sitting and crawling had been passed. Her mental development and language were consistent with that of a child her age. Nevertheless, my maternal instinct that something was wrong did not diminish.

By the time Lisa was twelve months old, she could pull herself up to a standing position and walk around holding onto the furniture, but she never took those first baby steps on her own. Whenever she sat in her baby walker it was clear that something just wasn't right. She propelled herself along the floor with her feet turned inwards at the ankles. Instead of putting her weight on the soles of her feet, she walked on the outer edge.

Lisa's hands were another cause for concern; her fingers were beginning to curl into the shape of a claw. Fortunately, we had an excellent health visitor. Penny was friendly and supportive and kept an eye on Lisa's progress.

Looking for answers I took Lisa to see Dr Twigg, a wise and experienced man who had been my family's GP for three generations.

I was apprehensive as I explained my concerns to him.

'Lisa's fingers are bent and I'm concerned about the way she walks.' I tried to put on a brave front.

'Let's see her walking, shall we?' he said.

I placed my daughter on the floor and held her hands firmly as I walked her up and down the room.

Dr Twigg nodded. 'I see what you mean.'

He examined her hands. 'I think we need to investigate this a bit more, don't you? I'll make arrangements for Lisa to see an orthopaedic consultant at the hospital to take a look at her muscles and joints. Let's wait and see what he has to say, and then we'll take it from there. OK?'

Having to wait more than a month for Lisa's hospital appointment wasn't easy. I had mixed feelings; I wanted to know but I was afraid of what I might find out.

When the day finally arrived, Jonathan couldn't get the time off work and I took Lisa on the bus for the ten-minute journey to hospital.

As we walked through the door into the outpatients' department, a sea of faces turned towards us. Amongst the crowd were adults and children with plaster casts on various limbs, and others were bandaged. Sitting on a cold plastic chair, I pulled Lisa's buggy in front so she was facing me. Seated opposite us was a very pale child, sitting beside his even paler mother. On the far side of the waiting area, a nurse pushed an elderly gentleman in a wheelchair, parked him against the wall and turned and walked away, leaving him on his own. He seemed confused and unaware of what was going on. The entrance doors opened and a middle-aged man hobbled in wearing a torn rugby shirt and muddy shorts, grimacing from an apparent knee injury.

Lisa looked up at me as if to say, 'What are we doing here, Mummy?' All I could do was smile reassuringly and try to make her believe everything was going to be all right, even if I wasn't sure it was.

Two hours, three children's picture books and two drinks later, a nurse called Lisa's name and I followed the blue uniform through a set of double doors into a large room with desks on either side. Men in white coats rushed in and out, engrossed in patients' medical notes. Seated to my right was a suited man in his early fifties. After a quick glance in my direction he returned to his notes and, without looking up, motioned for me to take a seat adjacent to his desk. His offhand manner made me feel uncomfortable. He introduced himself as Mr Oswell, and proceeded to launch into a barrage of questions. I made the mistake of referring to him as 'doctor' and was instantly corrected with a curt, 'It's Mr Oswell. I'm a consultant, not a doctor.' Being rebuked was the last thing I needed.

Without hesitation, the consultant-not-a-doctor launched into my medical history, asking, 'Did you have a normal pregnancy?' and 'Was it a normal delivery?'

I replied with a brief summary.

He took notes and nodded.

I explained my concerns. 'Lisa is over twelve months old, but can only walk if she is holding onto something; and when she does walk, her feet bend inwards at the ankles.'

I also enquired about the shape of her hands.

He gave Lisa a physical examination and then turned to me.

'There is a slight weakness in her ankles but they'll become stronger the more she walks.' He continued. 'I think you're overreacting, like first-time mothers often do.'

And that was that. This 'overanxious mother' was left with no other choice but to take her daughter home. Nothing had changed. I still had lots of questions . . . but no answers.

During the next few months, I paid two more visits to our GP to express my ongoing concerns about Lisa. Subsequently, an appointment was made with the same orthopaedic consultant at the hospital. Each time he gave the same response, 'It's nothing to worry about.'

After our third appointment with Mr Oswell (a fruitless exercise), Dr Twigg referred Lisa to the hospital's children's unit on the outskirts of town and arrangements were made for her to be admitted for the day to undergo tests.

I was going to get my answers.

They were going to turn my world upside down.

CHAPTER FOUR

The Diagnosis

The children's unit had as much charm as a six-inch hypodermic needle. The Transylvanian-style building was better suited to a horror movie than a hospital – an old, grey, two-storey building with exposed Tudor beams and long sash windows. There were probably bats in the attic too. Chimneys pointed like bony fingers up to the foreboding sky, and ominous storm clouds added to the gloom.

As Lisa and I walked in through the large wooden doors, away from the freezing wind's icy tentacles, something grabbed at my throat. It was that awful hospital smell of disinfectant which not only eradicated all known germs, but deterred friends and family from visiting loved ones.

The ward sister, wearing a dark-blue uniform and white cap, marched up to us, her ornate silver belt-buckle glinting with authority. With just a hint of a smile, she instructed, 'Come with me.' I followed her into the children's ward, pushing Lisa in her buggy. My daughter had a quizzical look but at that point I knew as little as she did.

The internal décor of the ward was bland. Over the years, white-painted walls had become off-coloured. Along the left-hand side stood a row of hospital beds, each with a faded orange curtain pulled to one side. In the centre of the ward, a row of small tables and chairs made of bright red plastic brought a much-needed splash of colour into the room, as did a few toys, scattered here and there. Along the right-hand wall stood a row of cots, little faces peering through the grey metal bars as if imprisoned, while mothers stood sentry beside their young.

The nursing sister led us to a cot at the far corner of the ward. I was grateful not to be placed in the middle of the row. My focus was on Lisa and I was trying to hold it all together. Isolated from any source of comfort or support, and with Jonathan at work, I felt very alone. Maybe I gave the appearance that I was coping and in control, but I was afraid of what the test results might show. Nevertheless, I had to know, one way or the other.

My daughter gazed up at me. Taking a firm grip of the cold impersonal bars of the metal cot, all I could do was smile in the hope of conveying, 'Don't worry, I'm here. I'm not going to leave you.'

At the far end of the ward, the double doors swung open and a cluster of white coats glided in for the doctor's obligatory ward round. The consultant and his entourage swiftly made their way from one bed to the next.

And then it was our turn.

The consultant paediatrician introduced himself as Mr Libbers. There was a flurry of papers as the team, which included two doctors, three medical students, the ward sister and a staff nurse, read my daughter's notes and then talked amongst one another as if Lisa and I were invisible.

I thought, 'She's my daughter; why don't you ask me about her?'

Turning to me at last, Mr Libbers fired off the same list of queries I had answered before.

'Tell me about your pregnancy. Did you go full-term? How long were you in labour? Was it a normal delivery? Were there any complications?'

The consultant performed a physical examination on Lisa, commenting to his team as he did so, and then moved on to the next patient.

The ward round complete, the white coats exited. My mind was racing. All I could think about was my labour, visualising each contraction forcing the back of my baby's skull against my pelvic bone because my cervix refused to dilate and let her descend into the birth canal. I couldn't help wondering if Lisa had suffered brain damage as a result. If so, was it my fault?

The next task was to take a sample of Lisa's bodily fluids to be tested. No one informed me what Lisa was being tested for or why. A friendly woman arrived, inserted a needle into Lisa's arm and drew some blood.

An hour later a young nurse informed me that she needed to take a urine sample from Lisa.

A bustle of activity in the centre of the ward indicated it was time for lunch. Toys were removed from tables and replaced with knives and forks. Women and children came and sat at the tables. Adults had to make do with sitting on child-sized chairs. The doors opened and the aroma of chips wafted into the ward, followed by the sound of a rattling trolley. There was a distinct lack of conversation around the meal table, yet everyone shared a common bond – our children had a reason for being there, whether to undergo tests, receive treatment, or have an operation. A couple of nurses joined the group and helped to feed children whose parents were absent. Their jovial manner helped to initiate dialogue around the table. When mealtime was over, the cutlery and dishes were exchanged for a variety of toys and games.

That afternoon the doctors returned. The consultant paediatrician cast his gaze around the ward and strode towards me, still sat on the small kiddie chair at the table beside Lisa. The white coats stood in a semicircle around me. I felt vulnerable, defenceless and completely at their mercy. Mr Libbers grabbed a child's chair and sat beside me. Suddenly the mothers who were sat around the table stood up and scattered in all directions, taking their children with them. Maybe they could sense what was coming.

I had been searching for an explanation for Lisa's condition for over a year and the time had finally arrived. Bracing myself for the impending news, I wished that Jonathan was there with me.

Time stood still and everything seemed to be moving in slow motion.

As I waited, the silence was deafening.

Without a second thought, I picked Lisa up and sat her on my lap in a vain attempt to protect her; but from what?

Mr Libbers dropped the diagnostic bomb I had been expecting since the day Lisa was born.

As he spoke, all I heard were the words 'spastic' and 'special school'.

They pierced my heart like ice-cold shrapnel.

In just one fragment of time, my hopes and dreams for Lisa's future were blasted into oblivion.

CHAPTER FIVE

Meeting God in the Toilet

At first, I felt totally overwhelmed and then a surge of anger rose within me. I was angry at the way I had been informed of my daughter's condition – in the middle of a hospital ward in full view of everyone. The consultant bore the full force of my emotions and I yelled in anguish, 'You bastard!' I leapt to my feet, the small kiddie chair flying backwards across the floor. I picked up my daughter, rushed to her cot and placed her inside, then ran out of the ward. The white coats were clearly startled by my outburst, except for the consultant, who appeared relatively unmoved.

Desperate for somewhere private to be alone, I fled into a nearby ladies' toilet. I was relieved to see there was only one cubicle and, darting inside, I rammed the lock closed in an attempt to shut out the rest of the world. I felt like my mind had been hijacked.

My daughter was *disabled*!

I wanted to scream but no words came out. I collided head-on with the full force of the shock, hopelessness and horror. I was desperately afraid. My soul felt like a punchbag and my insides, black-and-blue. I wanted to run away but my legs wouldn't move.

Then the tears came. My stoic façade vanished and any hint of self-control evaporated as I sobbed uncontrollably.

I cried until I began to feel empty and the tears slowly began to ebb away.

I stood there for a couple of minutes, exhausted and weary beyond measure. I knew that I should return to Lisa. I looked at my watch. I had been locked in there over two hours. My daughter needed her mummy but I had nothing left to give. All that remained was an overwhelming sense of helplessness. There was nothing I could do to save my daughter.

I wasn't sure whether God existed or not, but if there was a God then I needed Him right there and then. In weakness and desperation, I whispered, 'God, help me.'

Moments later the atmosphere became incredibly still and the toilet cubicle was filled with a tangible presence. Somehow, I knew it was God. It was like arriving home after a storm and being enfolded in a warm duvet in front of a log fire. What I can only describe as divine strength and power filled my soul. It eased my mind and restored my body. I felt completely transformed and filled to the brim with strength, hope and courage. From somewhere deep within, I knew that I was not alone any more.

There came a gentle tapping on the toilet door, followed by a warm voice enquiring, 'Are you all right, dear?'

Tentatively sliding back the bolt, I opened the door to see who it was.

'I work in the kitchen next door,' said the hospital orderly, her voice tender. 'I could hear you crying through the wall. Would you like me to make you a cup of tea?'

I nodded.

My Good Samaritan led me out of the toilet and into the hospital kitchen, and sat me down on a stool beside a stainless-steel worktop. Glad to have something to lean on, the kindness provided by the hospital orderly, together with a mug of hot sweet tea, was just what I needed.

The next face I saw was my mother's. She had received a phone call from the hospital requesting that she come to collect me and Lisa. I suddenly realised that I had been absent from Lisa for over three hours! I stood to my feet, said 'thank you' to my comforting angel, and quickly returned to the ward. A nurse was holding Lisa, who appeared to be OK and seemingly none the worse for having been deserted by me.

My mother then informed me, 'The consultant wants to see you in his office. He said it's important.'

Without saying a word, the nurse handed Lisa to me. After collecting our belongings from beside the cot, I pushed Lisa's buggy down the long corridor towards the consultant's office. My mother was curious, to say the least. 'What's happened?'

After a brief summary of the day's events, I calmly reassured her, 'I'm all right, Mum. God's with me.'

She didn't say a word. Maybe she thought I had lost my mind.

I knocked on the consultant's door and, upon hearing 'come in', we entered the room. Mr Libbers sat behind his desk and invited us to take a seat opposite him. The afternoon sun filtered through orange curtains, created a warm and soothing glow. I lifted my daughter out of her buggy and placed her on her grandmother's lap.

The consultant paediatrician fixed his gaze upon me and, in a gentle tone of voice, enquired, 'How are you?'

My earlier outburst was very out of character for me and I felt a little embarrassed. I replied sheepishly, 'I'm OK. Sorry for swearing at you.' He nodded as if to accept my apology.

He then looked me straight in the eye and said, 'We have completed our tests and have the results.' He paused for a few moments. 'I'm afraid I have some bad news for you.'

I looked across at my mother, whose eyes were fixed on Mr Libbers, and felt grateful for her company. Preoccupied with a picture book, Lisa was seemingly oblivious to the gravity of our conversation.

This was it.

A few seconds ticked by, but it felt like an eternity.

After fifteen months of waiting and wondering, I was informed that Lisa had a rare nerve disorder with progressive muscle wasting, starting in her hands and feet and gradually working its way up her body until it reached the vital organs. There was no cure. My daughter would gradually waste away.

I felt like I had been hit by a truck on the motorway, sent hurtling across the central barrier, and then crashed head-on with another truck.

Three generations of my family walked out of the children's unit that day with barely a word spoken between them. Unable to face going home straightaway, I asked my mother if she could take us to my father's house, which she did.

Carrying Lisa in my arms, I walked into the lounge where my father was standing by the fireplace. All I could manage to say was a brief 'hi' and dropped onto the settee. My father resumed his conversation with his wife, Carol. It didn't take long before he realised that something was wrong. Carol must have sensed it too and said, 'Come on, Lisa, let's go into the kitchen and find a biscuit, shall we?' Lisa smiled in agreement and exited the room in Carol's arms.

Slowly pulling myself to my feet, I went to my father. Born in former Yugoslavia he had relocated to the UK as a young man and was now a successful insurance broker. Strong, caring and wise, my father was my port in a storm.

Opening his arms wide, I leaned into him, grateful for somewhere to rest my weary head and battered heart. Safe and secure in my father's embrace, I began to weep and then I broke the news.

'Lisa's dying.'

A solitary tear fell down my father's cheek.

CHAPTER SIX

The London Hospital

Telling Jonathan was never going to be easy. At first, he couldn't take it in, and then we sat and wept together. A kind friend offered us their caravan to use free of charge. Situated in the corner of a remote field in the midst of the countryside, it was exactly what we needed – a chance to get away from it all with our beautiful fifteen-month-old daughter, who in spite of the fact she was dying, seemed very much alive.

For the next few days our refuge-on-wheels provided shelter in our storm-tossed world.

A follow-up appointment was made for Lisa to attend a major teaching hospital in London that specialised in paediatric neuromuscular diseases and had a worldwide reputation for their advances in clinical research. I was grateful Jonathan was able to come with us on that occasion.

When we arrived at the hospital, we made our way to the children's outpatient department. This was the first time we had been in hospital since receiving the heart-breaking news about Lisa. I felt a strange mixture of acceptance and denial.

Entering the department was like stepping into a world with a one-way ticket. The waiting area was heaving with adults, most of whom were women, sat around the edge of the room while their children played in the centre.

Brightly painted walls displayed a jungle scene of trees, vines and long grass, with various animals enjoying their habitat.

Although the room resembled a play area, it had one major difference – a varied collection of walking aids, wheelchairs and oxygen tanks, plus that dreadful aroma of disinfectant which clung stubbornly to the air.

Eventually, a seat became available and I sat down, trying to take it all in. A young teenage girl sat in a wheelchair, propped up by cushions. A small child sat on his father's lap, happily swinging his callipered legs to and fro. Some children walked with an unusual gait; others wore hearing aids. Toys were strewn everywhere and brothers and sisters played with their disabled siblings.

Parents sat gazing into the distance. There seemed to be a mutual respect amongst the adults and everyone could sense when someone didn't want to talk. We possessed a language that required no articulation. People's facial expressions spoke volumes, ranging from 'a bit tired' to 'totally worn out'. Occasionally tensions bubbled over, a parent yelling at their child, 'I said stop it!'

The full reality of our future was right before my eyes. There was no escaping it. 'Life before Lisa' was relatively carefree and without complication. Now, our lives were full of challenges and changes.

After an hour of waiting, a nurse called out Lisa's name. Compared to the jungle scene, this room's décor was bland. There were no colourful murals, just a few posters stuck on magnolia-painted walls, a chart depicting the normal growth and development of a child, plus a collection of images promoting the benefits of healthy nutrition. The room was sparsely furnished: one desk, a few chairs and a table. A vertical ruler against one wall measured a child's height, and on the floor below a set of footprints indicated where to place their feet. On the table were weighing scales for babies and toddlers. Older children stood on floor scales, their weight displayed using a counterbalance.

The nurse asked some routine questions about our daughter, including her date of birth. Lisa was by now eighteen months old. She was weighed, her height measured and the relevant data written in a hospital file. After the general check-up, we were instructed to return to the waiting area and rejoin the queue to see the doctor or consultant assigned to the clinic that day. These were members of 'The Muscle Team'.

After another short wait, it was our turn again. Seated behind a desk, the doctor studied Lisa's file containing notes from our GP and test results from the children's unit where I had received the initial diagnosis. Once again, I was asked questions about my pregnancy with Lisa and her delivery.

The doctor continued his line of enquiry.

'Have you taken Lisa to the baby clinic for her routine development checks? Were her sight and hearing tested?'

'Yes,' I replied. 'And the results were normal.'

I explained that Lisa was unable to walk independently and needed to hold onto something. I described how she walked on the outside edge of her feet instead of the soles.

The doctor performed a thorough physical examination but was unable to provide us with any further information. Past doctors and consultants had been rather stiff and starchy but this doctor was different; he had an amicable nature, which made him approachable.

Three months later Lisa and I returned to London for her general check-up, and once again I felt apprehensive. This time we would meet the professor. The moment we entered his office, he looked up from his desk and greeted us with a warm, 'Hello, please take a seat.' I liked him and felt at ease. Here was a professional who did not reside in 'Airs and Graces Castle' but instead seemed more like a compassionate grandfather figure.

Alongside the professor were men and women from his medical team who, after a brief introduction, proceeded to discuss Lisa's case. The professor included me in the conversation and took the time to explain some of the medical terms so that I could understand what they were talking about. His kind and thoughtful manner had a direct impact on the way I felt about Lisa's diagnosis, not to mention any possible outcome. I no longer felt quite so alone and I wasn't being treated like a neurotic mother.

Two years had passed since Lisa's birth, and at long last I had a name for her condition.

'Peripheral neuropathy.'

Having peripheral neuropathy means that one or more of the peripheral nerves are damaged, which consequently affects the transmission of messages sent from the brain to the rest of the body. In Lisa's case, when the electrochemical message left her brain, the signal was strong, but by the time it reached the end of its journey, it had fizzled out along the way, indicating a problem with her motor nerve conduction. Lisa's muscles were not receiving the proper instructions to move, which resulted in a loss of muscle tissue and muscle wasting.

Up to that point, Lisa didn't seem to be experiencing any loss of sensation in her hands and feet, nor did she complain of any discomfort or pain in her lower limbs.

Our local hospital's orthopaedic consultant had informed me that Lisa's weak ankles would strengthen as she walked.

But I never got to experience the pleasure of seeing my daughter take those first baby steps without someone holding onto her.

CHAPTER SEVEN

Lisa Goes to School

I approached the main entrance of the school for children with special needs, in a neighbouring town, with a heavy heart. The assortment of walking aids, wheelchairs and specially adapted chairs hit me like a sudden icy blast on a winter's day. With nowhere to run and nowhere to hide, any lingering denial was forcefully evicted. As I stood in reception trying to take it all in, the words *'Disabled! Disabled! Disabled!'* pounded on the door of my heart.

I had arrived ten minutes early for my appointment with the headteacher. I noticed a collection of photographs on the wall and went to have a closer look. I assumed these photos depicted children within the school; they seemed to have all sorts of disabilities, most of which I had never seen before. They looked vastly different from Lisa, who at first glance didn't look physically disabled, especially when sat in her buggy.

Staff and children were engaged in their classroom activities. It seemed very quiet for a school environment. Then I realised what it was. I couldn't hear any children laughing.

A man in a suit walked towards me and assuming him to be the headteacher, I instantly applied the 'I'm fine' mask and steeled myself for whatever might be coming next. The man introduced himself as Mr Morris, offered a warm handshake and led me to his office. He gave me a brief description of the school and then we discussed the best way forward for Lisa. A tour of the premises followed, my despondency concealed under a whitewashed smile.

The classrooms were a hive of activity. The children had mental and physical disabilities which ranged from moderate to severe. Some of the children appeared able-bodied and communicated without any difficulty, which had me puzzled.

As I walked along the corridor, a boy of approximately nine years of age strode past using crutches. His gait was unusual, swinging from side to side, both legs turned outwards at the knee. The boy smiled at us and gave a cheery, 'Hello!'

These children were so happy!

Mr Morris escorted me into the physiotherapy room, the size of a small hall. Attached to the wall was a ladder climbing frame with thick wooden rungs, and upon the floor were large square mats. In the far corner was a large blue exercise ball. Various tricycles of different shapes and sizes were scattered around the room.

Further along the corridor we came to a door with 'School Nurse' written on it and after knocking gently, entered. The room had a friendly atmosphere, enhanced by soft mellow light streaming through the windows. A middle-aged lady wearing a tunic top greeted us with a smile.

I had expected to be confronted by all sorts of unusual sights and sounds, but the overall impression was much better than I had imagined. I was really impressed by the staff. Every team member – teachers, class assistants and volunteer helpers – seemed to work extremely hard in what I considered to be a challenging and yet rewarding environment.

The last port of call was the nursery. Along both sides of the cloakroom, small coats hung on wooden pegs, with an assortment of rucksacks and bags. Adjacent to the cloakroom were the nursery toilets. The play room was filled with colour and motion, with eight children engaged in various activities. A pink wooden dolls' house containing miniature furniture stood near the wall, and next to it a child's play oven, with white plastic pots and pans upon the hob and a young girl fully engrossed, concocting an imaginary meal. Children wearing bright plastic aprons were sat at the table and painting on large sheets of white paper. They were obviously having fun, with more yellow and green paint on the children than on the paper. The teacher and class assistants clearly had their hands full!

A little girl, approximately four years of age, sat on a heavy wooden chair specially adapted to meet her needs, with strong padded cushions providing extra support on the seat, back and sides of the chair, plus the armrests. A headrest with padded sides kept the girl's head in an upright position. Not having seen a chair like that before, I had no idea they even existed. A class assistant held a cup for the child to drink, its spouted lid preventing the juice from spilling.

Mr Morris introduced me to the person in charge of the nursery department. Mrs Gingham was clearly devoted to the children in her care, and it was reassuring to know that Lisa would be happy and safe in the school. My daughter would be attending full-time on weekdays.

Leaving the nursery, Mr Morris led us down an adjacent corridor and showed me the toilet facilities used by the older children, which at first glance were the same as any other. In a separate room across the corridor was a single toilet with a handrail beside it. Secured against the opposite wall was a platform which could be lowered for changing nappies. Similar in appearance to a nappy-changing room commonly found in shopping centres, this facility was used for older children, rather than babies. A ten-year-old child wearing nappies? It was certainly news to me! Some of the children were doubly incontinent too. I couldn't help admire class assistants who attended to the children's personal needs, day in and day out. It must take quite a bit of stamina, especially with older children who are undoubtedly much heavier.

It was a day like no other, filled with sights and sounds I had never encountered before – children between the ages of two and eleven whose bodies jerked uncontrollably, or were prone to sudden muscle spasms. Some were limp because of muscle weakness. Occasionally, a child cried out in frustration, unable to communicate what they wanted to say because their brain was trapped inside a body which seemed to have a mind of its own.

After my tour of the school I left feeling that the people who worked there were a very dedicated team, committed to a common goal: to help every child achieve their full potential.

When the day came for Lisa to go to the school, I had mixed feelings. She was a happy little girl at home and enjoyed playing with dolls and her teaset, handing me imaginary cups, which I pretended to drink. Her vivid imagination transformed cardboard boxes into trains, cars, boats and planes. She regularly brought me colourful storybooks to read aloud while we chatted about the pictures. I was hopeful that she would enjoy her new environment and make friends there, but I also felt uneasy because I was letting go of my little girl and placing her into the hands of people who I barely knew. Lisa was vulnerable and I felt inordinately protective of her.

When I took Lisa into the nursery she clung onto me for dear life. For the first couple of days, I stayed with Lisa until she began to get used to her new surroundings. Mrs Gingham assured me that Lisa would be OK after I had gone.

'Just tell her "goodbye, see you later" and smile as you go.'

Following the teacher's instructions, I reluctantly left my daughter in their capable hands. I hoped she would soon adjust to going to school every day. The school bus picked her up each morning and brought her home in the afternoon.

CHAPTER EIGHT

The Nativity

A few months after Lisa began to attend nursery, it became evident that she had developed a squint. One eye looked straight ahead and the other slightly inwards. She was given an eye patch to wear over the good eye for a few hours each day to encourage the weaker one to work harder, thereby correcting the problem.

An eye test also revealed that Lisa had astigmatism, an unevenly curved cornea producing slightly blurred vision. Spectacles were prescribed, and being the early 1980s, the range of NHS frames was pale pink for girls, or pale blue for boys.

At the same time, I noticed that when I called Lisa's name she didn't always respond. Periodic screening at the local baby and toddler clinic had not revealed any problems, and Lisa had passed the hearing tests. However, after Lisa's third birthday her hearing levels seemed to have changed. Just to make sure, I decided to test her hearing myself before taking matters further.

One afternoon when Lisa was engrossed in her favourite children's TV programme, I stood six feet behind and banged a saucepan lid with a wooden spoon. I was relieved when Lisa turned her head to see where the noise was coming from. A couple of minutes later I crept up behind her and whispered in her ear, but his time she didn't turn around. Taking two steps backwards, I spoke her name in a normal voice. Still no response. Clearly this was a matter for concern but I had absolutely no idea what to do next.

A few days later, the nursery teacher told me she needed to have a word with me and I paid her a visit. Taking me to one side, Mrs Gingham informed me that she wasn't happy with Lisa's general behaviour in class.

'When I ask Lisa to do something, she ignores me. She won't participate in any of our group sessions either.'

This confirmed my suspicions.

'I don't think she can hear you,' I said.

Mrs Gingham refused to accept my comments, stating that in her professional opinion, my daughter was unresponsive because she was lazy.

After this, arrangements were made for an educational psychologist to assess Lisa both at school and in her home environment. Educational psychologists are invaluable when it comes to understanding a child's development, their need for social interaction and knowing how to promote the child's well-being. They provide a valuable service consulting, advising and training schools and carers to help children progress through the various stages in their education. Melinda (assigned to Lisa) paid us a home visit and listened patiently while I spoke about my daughter. Over the next few months Melinda became better acquainted with my family. She was more than just another professional involved in Lisa's case; here was someone who was actually on our side.

Before the age of three, Lisa was able to feed and dress herself on her own. However, as the muscle weakness in her lower limbs progressed, simple everyday tasks became increasingly difficult for her to achieve and she required more help. It was much quicker to dress Lisa myself rather than wait for her to do it, which invariably took longer. On weekday mornings, I would dress Lisa to save time because she needed to be ready when the school bus arrived. One day I received a message from school informing me that Lisa had dressed herself. Realising that my daughter's independence was a crucial stage in her development, I made allowances for the extra time it took for Lisa to dress herself and encouraged her to do so, but with a little help from me now and then.

At Christmastime, the nursery was planning a school performance, and invitations had been sent to parents and friends. On the day itself, I was so depressed that I couldn't bear the thought of facing anyone. As far as I was aware, Lisa was not taking part and therefore I remained at home. Later that afternoon I received a phone call from Mrs Gingham at the school.

'Why didn't you come to the school play?' She was clearly miffed. 'We did the Nativity. Where were you?'

'I'm sorry. I wasn't feeling well. Was Lisa in it?'

'Lisa had a lead role! She was Mary, the mother of Jesus! She was looking everywhere for you!'

It felt like the bottom had dropped out of my world. Stunned, I could barely get my words out. 'Why didn't you *tell* me?'

Mrs Gingham had wanted it to be a surprise. Had I known beforehand, I would definitely have gone to the school, regardless of how I was feeling. I was so upset that she hadn't told me. But she was not to blame; it was I who chose not to go and selfishly put my own needs first. I should have been there, for Lisa's sake. I was gutted. The moment I put the phone down, something broke and I began to weep.

A moment once lost is lost forever.

As far as I was concerned, something priceless occurred that day and I was not there to witness it. Regret consumed me. When Lisa came home from school that afternoon she couldn't tell me about her lead role because her communication skills were limited, nor could she express how it felt when she realised that her mummy wasn't there to see it.

That day I made a vow that I would never miss a school performance again. I would go to every school play no matter what, and every sports' day come rain or shine. No matter how I felt, or whatever I was going through at the time, my daughter would always be more important to me than anything else.

The regret stayed with me for years.

When I get to heaven, I'll ask to see an action replay on the big screen.

I'll watch a timeless role, beautifully performed by an adorable little girl who needed to sit because she couldn't walk.

CHAPTER NINE

Statemented

'Has Lisa been statemented?' enquired one of her teachers.

'Has she been *what*?' I replied, with absolutely no idea what she was talking about.

Within multiple layers of the world of special needs, there is a vocabulary I would have to learn fast. Each disabled child had an Individual Education Plan (IEP) drawn up, compiled by their teachers, focusing on the child's literacy, language, maths, behaviour and social skills. Any special help given to the child was also stated, including the frequency of the provision and the person providing it. A child's personal targets and progress was also stated in the IEP. Specific ways in which a parent could help at home were addressed too.

Dropped into the uncharted waters of the Local Authority – a river of never-ending twists and turns, fraught with bureaucracy and red tape – I could either sink or swim. In the 1980s, the Local Authority (LA) carried out a detailed investigation known as a 'Statutory Assessment' to discover the specific needs of a child, and whether or not the school could meet those needs with the resources available. The LA needed to be informed if the child required further specialised help, and if so would obtain reports from the child's school, educational psychologist, and Local Health Authority (doctor), Social Services and anyone else involved in the child's case.

Parents' views or concerns were also taken into account; after all, they knew their child better than anyone else!

The Local Authority's SEN (Special Educational Needs) officers would then collect the information from the Statutory Assessment and, if necessary, write a 'Statement of Special Educational Needs'. This official document stated the child's specific needs and how they were to be met. Long-term aims, plus arrangements for setting short-term goals, were included in the statement, together with instructions to review and monitor the child's progress on a regular basis. Non-educational needs were also addressed using information provided by the Health Authority, Social Services, and any organisations deemed relevant.

I wish someone had told me about the whole statementing procedure before I went through it. If a child's statement failed to stipulate a particular need, then the LA was not duty-bound to provide the necessary resources to meet that need, and I had to learn the hard way. When realising that Lisa needed extra support at school, I approached a member of staff who informed me bluntly, 'It's not on her statement.' No doubt funding was an issue. Trying to get an official document changed was like trudging through treacle, but I don't give up easily.

Lisa's first statement was somewhat lacking, to say the least. After the statement was first issued it was subsequently rewritten, and by the *second* time around, I had gained a much clearer understanding regarding the importance of articulating my views in a very concise manner to ensure that Lisa's needs were fully met. The paperwork was detailed and complicated and if the statement was not worded correctly it could be fraught with loopholes, meaning that the LA could avoid making the required provision mandatory. Put in simple terms: if the statement did not say it, the LA did not have to provide it.

I had to learn how the system worked.

And, for Lisa's sake, I had to learn fast.

CHAPTER TEN

Red Boots and Ballet Shoes

Shoes are very important to a girl. When Lisa was a toddler she wore cute sandals of cream leather with pink patterned hearts and peek-a-boo toes. Her favourite shoes at the age of three were black patent leather ones with a T-bar. The weak muscles in her ankles meant that Lisa was unable to flex or extend both feet. Whenever she walked, her feet flopped downwards at the ankle, known as 'foot drop'. To prevent her toes from scraping along the ground, Lisa had to pick up her legs in a high-stepping action.

One day, when I tickled the soles of her feet I discovered that she couldn't feel anything. Her sensory nerves had fallen victim to the neurological disorder. The muscle weakness continued to progress until Lisa's shoes no longer provided the necessary support. An appointment was made at the London hospital to see an orthotist, a specialist in the design, manufacture and fitting of a brace or splint known as an orthosis, which helps to control, limit, or immobilise a part of the body and support weak limbs.

John Canali's professional yet friendly manner put me at ease straightaway. It was our first visit to the orthotist's treatment room in the London hospital. He sat Lisa on a bench, examined her legs and explained the purpose of a splint. A plaster cast would be made of each leg from the foot to the knee. The cast was sent to a workshop in another location where the splints were constructed. Made of strong plastic, each L-shaped brace (an Ankle Foot Orthosis, or AFO) would go under the soles of both feet and surround the back of the lower leg. The splint covered the ankle joint on both sides, continued around the calf and fastened at the front with a Velcro strap, just under the knee. The splint would give her ankles greater stability and prevent foot drop. The foot and ankle section would fit snugly inside her shoes too.

Up on the wall of Mr Canali's treatment room was a print of a grand yacht with large white sails, coursing through azure seas on a clear summer's day. Whenever I saw the yacht, it evoked a longing to escape to a remote desert island far away from the endless heartache I kept hidden beneath the surface.

A couple of weeks later, we returned to London to collect Lisa's new AFOs. The splints undoubtedly helped, but seeing my daughter walk with fixed rigid ankles was something I would have to get used to. Fortunately, Lisa didn't seem to mind. Wearing thin, knee-high socks beneath the splints prevented skin chafing. At least I could pull the socks up to cover the Velcro straps, which made the splints less noticeable.

As Lisa grew older she wore trainers more often, which apparently were the preferred style of footwear for AFOs. Whenever I put Lisa's shoes on, her toes would curl downwards and I had to slip my finger into the shoe to straighten her toes. Sometimes when other people put Lisa's shoes on, they didn't realise that her toes were bent inside. It must have been so uncomfortable for her to have her toes scrunched up all day.

Disabled children are rarely asked to be bridesmaids. However, when planning their wedding my brother, John, and his fiancée, Kelly, thought it would be wonderful to have his four-year-old niece as a bridesmaid. Sophia, another bridesmaid, would be directly behind Lisa as they walked down the aisle, keeping a firm grip on her hands so she wouldn't fall over. Kelly had asked if Lisa could wear cream silk ballet shoes on the day, and without her splints too. Of course, I was absolutely delighted for Lisa to be a bridesmaid, but I had my reservations. For Lisa to walk down the aisle without her splints and strong leather shoes to support her ankles – I wasn't sure if she could manage it. But Kelly was insistent and I finally agreed. After all, it's not every day a girl gets to be a bridesmaid!

Lisa's outfit was stunning. Made of luxurious cream silk, the dress had a fitted bodice, short puffed sleeves, and a crinoline underskirt for extra volume, plus white tights. The headdress was a simple narrow headband, overlaid with silk ribbon and interspersed with tiny pearls to match those sewn delicately by hand onto the dress.

On the day of the wedding, the sun shone and my daughter looked like a princess. As the guests assembled in the chapel, the light streamed through colourful stained-glass windows. I placed Lisa into the capable hands of Sophia, made my way to a pew near the front and sat beside the aisle, not wanting to miss a single moment. My brother stood at the front, adjusting his attire for the umpteenth time, waiting for his bride to arrive.

A burst of classical melody brought a wave of anticipation and excitement. The assembled guests stood to their feet and turned towards the main entrance, straining their necks to catch a glimpse of the bridesmaids and bride, who with slow and methodical steps, made their way down the aisle towards the altar.

And then I saw her . . .

My daughter looked adorable, her rich brunette hair kissed by the sun and glistening with natural gold highlights.

Sophia walked immediately behind Lisa, bending slightly forwards over my four-year-old to keep her upright. Having foot drop, Lisa had to pick her knees up higher than normal to prevent her toes from scraping along the flagstone floor. She seemed unsure of each step but she managed to walk in flimsy ballet shoes and without splints.

As my precious daughter came closer and closer to the altar, I could see the concentration and effort etched across her face. I was overwhelmed by the sight of my beautiful angel.

My little girl appeared to be searching the crowd, looking for her mummy. I was determined not to cry. When Lisa finally reached me, she looked up and smiled as if to say, 'I did it!' I picked her up and sat her on my lap. I gave her a big hug. I could not have been prouder of my brave little girl in her ballgown and ballet shoes.

The inevitable day arrived when Lisa could no longer wear normal shoes and required special orthotic shoes instead. Designed for children with a disability, they provided maximum support to the ankles. The first time I laid eyes on the new footwear my heart sank. The clumpy leather ankle boots were black and blue and laced down the front. I thought they were the ugliest boots I had ever seen!

Thankfully, in due course someone realised that disabled children needed footwear that would not be hidden in the back of a wardrobe, or buried under a bed, or accidentally 'lost' by a disgruntled child who just didn't want to wear them. Piedro® boots were a vast improvement on anything I had seen before. Not only were the designers aware of the need for purpose-made boots, it seemed they took into account the child's feelings too. The strong leather ankle boots provided the necessary ankle support that Lisa needed. Her feet were measured and the boots ordered.

Lisa's Piedros ensured that her feet and ankles were held in the correct position while standing and walking. Putting the boots on proved much easier than her previous footwear; the laces went further down the front and by loosening them I could pull the boot open with plenty of room to slide my finger underneath Lisa's foot to pull her toes straight. The boots were ideal for children who wore AFOs. My daughter looked quite trendy in her red leather boots. Other children seemed to like them too, which made it easier for her to fit in with her able-bodied peers instead of standing out like a sore thumb.

As the muscle weakness continued to progress it soon became apparent that Lisa needed extra support for her lower legs, and from now on would have to wear calipers instead of her AFOs.

Attached to either side of the Piedro boot was a thick metal bar which continued up the lower leg to a horizontal strap just below the knee. The first time I saw Lisa's calipers it was like being punched in the gut by a welterweight boxer. While struggling with the fact that my daughter needed to wear calipers, there was no denying the truth. The bright red boots with heavy metal calipers and red strap was like a trumpet blasting out one unavoidable message: 'My child is disabled!'

Every time I pushed Lisa to the shops in her buggy people would stare at her. Children were far easier to cope with than adults because they would simply enquire, 'What's wrong with her legs?' I preferred the direct and honest approach. When I told the children, 'Her legs are weak and she can't walk on her own,' they simply responded, 'Oh' and walked away.

But this wasn't all. Not only did I have a four-year-old child with a progressive muscle wasting condition, it seemed that my daughter was losing her hearing as well. Without any clue where to go or what to do next, I took Lisa to see our GP and an appointment was made for a hearing test. My suspicions confirmed, Lisa was then sent to an Ear, Nose and Throat consultant (ENT) in the next county who diagnosed her with glue ear, a common condition in children.

With glue ear, a thick sticky fluid has collected in the middle ear canal behind the eardrum, impeding the small bones from transmitting to the inner ear, and therefore hearing is impaired. Lisa needed to be admitted to hospital to have a grommet inserted into each eardrum – a small tube to drain fluid from the middle ear. The procedure was to be carried out under a general anaesthetic.

As always, my daughter was a little star. Whilst Lisa was in theatre I waited anxiously at her bedside, hoping and praying that she would return in one piece. The operation only took around thirty minutes and I was so relieved to see her again.

It must have been a strange experience for my daughter. At first, she seemed groggy and felt queasy from the anaesthetic, but the effects soon wore off and she remained in hospital overnight for observation.

I was relieved when Lisa's hearing appeared to improve. A few months later, both grommets fell out and her eardrums healed over.

But my sense of relief was short-lived.

Lisa's hearing continued to deteriorate. I was now faced with another mountain to climb. I had no choice but to keep moving forward because there was no going back. In spite of it all, there was something about Lisa which kept me going.

Just a glimpse of her indomitable spirit caused me to look upon our Mount Everest and convince myself, 'I can do this' even if it meant suffering a few bumps and bruises along the way.

CHAPTER ELEVEN

Baby James

The thought of having another child with special needs was more than I could bear. If Jonathan and I were to have a second child, would they have the same illness as Lisa? Knowing that my child's condition would deteriorate was like having a bad toothache which flared up every now and then. At times, the pain in my soul would catch me off-guard and make me wince. Taking a few painkillers of denial took the edge off and provided a modicum of relief, but it was only short term. Did I really have both the mental and emotional capacity to take on even more?

Seeking wise counsel and professional guidance, an appointment was made for my husband and me to see a genetic counsellor at the London hospital. Questions were asked regarding our families' medical history.

Were there any cases of muscle weakness?

Unable to recollect anything in our current or previous generations, Jonathan did mention a member of his family who had muscle weakness in his ankles. The counsellor asked us to investigate further and a follow-up appointment was made.

Not wanting to apportion blame to any member of his family, Jonathan approached his mother and carefully made enquiries regarding the man concerned, but she refused to discuss the matter. The last thing Jonathan and I wanted to do was point the finger at anyone. We were merely looking for answers and trying to figure out where to go from there.

Over the next few weeks all sorts of questions went through my mind:

Was I the cause?

Was it Jonathan?

Did both of us carry a recessive gene?

Did my husband's family pass it on, or had it come from my side of the family?

Trying to navigate my way through feelings of blame and guilt was like walking across a rickety old rope bridge stretched across a deep ravine. While unsure of my footing, I knew I had to keep going in order to reach the other side. Hopefully my husband and I would make it safely across together.

In our follow-up appointment with the genetic counsellor, we presented our findings – or lack of – about Jonathan's side of the family, including the person with weak ankles. Unable to see any concrete evidence, the counsellor informed us that in her professional opinion, our daughter's condition was probably caused by a 'mutant gene'. Some of the genetic material passed on to Lisa had become altered in some way, resulting in a permanent change in the gene's function. It was deemed highly unlikely that any future children of ours would be similarly affected.

I had mixed emotions. Although relieved that Jonathan and I had been given the 'all clear' to have another child, I was now faced with the prospect of having to go through the process of childbirth again. My previous labour had resulted in deep emotional scars which I kept hidden from everyone, including Jonathan. Sorely disappointed at my inability to produce a child by normal delivery, I had felt robbed of what should have been a unique experience for us as a couple. To top it all, Lisa had come into the world while I was under general anaesthetic and I therefore missed the opportunity to bond with my child immediately after her birth.

When I became pregnant with our second child, I was delighted but apprehensive. Although we had received the 'all clear' from the counsellor, there was still a nagging doubt in the back of my mind. Would I experience the same awareness that something was wrong as I had when Lisa was born?

It was a relief, when I went into labour, to find my baby's back was not lying against mine, and therefore I didn't suffer from horrible back pain with every contraction. Unfortunately, however, my body seemed to be following the same pattern as before, and when I tried to explain this to the doctor on the labour ward, he dismissed it and went off duty. Amidst my frustration, I had no other choice but to spend the next few hours in unproductive labour.

Eventually, when the doctor returned he informed me that because I had been in labour for eleven hours with no sign of baby's arrival, I was deemed 'failure to progress'. Resisting the urge to say, 'I told you so,' I was taken to theatre for a Caesarean section. Once again, I had been denied the experience of having a normal delivery.

Jonathan and I became the proud parents of a gorgeous baby boy, weighing seven pounds fourteen ounces. We named him James on his birth certificate, but called him Jamie. The first time I held my son there wasn't even a hint that something was wrong, and what a relief it was! Jamie appeared perfectly normal in every way.

Our four-year-old daughter took to Jamie straight away and often included him when playing with her toys. She would pretend to read her picture-storybooks to Jamie and presented her valued collection of Barbie dolls for his approval. Our daughter protected her younger sibling as if he were a fragile new puppy. It was the beginning of a precious relationship between an amazing little girl and her brother, whom she adored.

CHAPTER TWELVE

See John

An important meeting was scheduled at my daughter's school but I had been stricken with a virus, my nerve endings inflamed and every movement painful. In the hope of regaining some mobility, I took some extra-strong painkillers to relieve the symptoms. Unfortunately, they didn't help and I had to resign myself to the fact that I wouldn't be able to attend the meeting to discuss Lisa's progress.

That afternoon, my elder brother, John, and his wife, Kelly, made an impromptu visit to my home. John had become a 'born-again Christian' a few months previously and the change in his persona was quite a surprise to those who knew him. Shortly after his conversion, John paid our mother a visit, carrying a Bible tucked under his arm and enthusing about Jesus as if he knew Him personally. My mother was bemused, to say the least, if not slightly cynical, that her son, who as a teenager was prone to the occasional volatile outburst, was now happy and smiling! Clearly something had happened to him, but what?

After 'jovial John' had said his goodbyes and left, Mother turned to me and with a wry grin remarked, 'He's clearly lost his marbles!'

Struck by the obvious change in my brother's demeanour, I couldn't help thinking, 'He hasn't lost his mind – he's happy!'

John could see that I was in a lot of pain and asked, 'Would you like us to pray for you?' It was the first time someone had offered to pray for me and to be honest, I felt a bit awkward, but I was desperate and acquiesced. My brother and his wife put their hands on my shoulder, prayed a short and simple prayer asking Jesus to heal me, and that was that. After chatting for a while over tea and cake, they said 'cheerio' and left.

Ten minutes later the pain suddenly left my body. Just to make sure, I moved my arms and legs and then turned my head from side to side as far as it would go. The pain and discomfort had completely disappeared.

There was no doubt about it, I had been miraculously healed!

I suddenly realised that the same Jesus who healed people 2,000 years ago is still alive and healing people today!

Completely recovered and re-energised, I drove to Lisa's school and arrived just in time to attend the meeting about my daughter's future.

A few days later, in order to make absolutely certain that God was real, I decided to put Him to the test.

Lisa had developed contractures in both hands, a shortening of the muscles and tendons which caused her fingers to bend. To help prevent the contractures from worsening, I had to gently straighten her fingers one by one on a regular basis, but the moment I released each finger it would immediately curl towards her palm again. Lisa's hands also felt cold to the touch most of the time. After putting my daughter to bed one night, I spoke these words: 'God, if You're real, touch Lisa!'

The next morning, when I walked into my daughter's bedroom, I found her stiffened fingers were no longer bent but perfectly straight! Taking her hands in mine, each finger was relaxed and supple. Her hands were no longer cold but warm. That was more than my human brain could cope with, and to be honest it freaked me out!

'OK, God, that's enough!' I said, needing Him to back off for a while.

A few weeks later my brother gave me a book entitled *When the Spirit Comes*,[1] by Colin Urquhart. The book recounted modern-day accounts of people in the congregation who had been physically healed by the power of God, as well as various miracles in the local community. Never before had I seen or heard anything like it. Over the next few weeks I began to sense that God was drawing me closer to Himself. Intrigued, I began compiling a list of questions in my mind, until one day I was so frustrated that I blurted out, 'God, show me what to do!' Moments later I received an instruction.

'See John.'

It was April and I was about to realise that Easter wasn't about chocolate eggs and fluffy bunnies. At the time my brother was overseas on a business trip and I had to wait three weeks before we could meet up, by which time I was almost bursting at the seams in my quest for answers! Standing in John's kitchen, I poured out the long list of questions that I had accumulated. My brother looked rather taken aback, and with a big smile said, 'Whoa, slow down!' Reaching for his Bible, John addressed my questions one by one.

For the first time in my life I began to understand what the cross was all about. God did not send Jesus to *condemn* the world but to *save* it.[2] I had spent my life trying to make it on my own. A wall of self-protection meant 'no one in and no one out'. It was far safer that way, or so I thought. But I was isolated from the one person who could help me the most.

Suddenly, everything became crystal-clear. I couldn't turn my back on Him any more. I used to go to Sunday school as a child, so I thought I knew a bit about Jesus, but no one

---

1. Hodder & Stoughton, 1974.
2. See John 3:17.

told me that you can actually have a *relationship* with God! Believing the Bible to be true, I was ready to take the next step.

My brother and I relocated to the lounge and sat on the sofa, Kelly to my left, John to my right, and me in the middle.

There was nothing religious about it, which suited me just fine.

Holding John and Kelly's hands, I said a simple prayer.

Minutes later I experienced what felt like blocks of concrete being lifted out of me. Although I didn't understand what was happening, it didn't matter because it felt really good. An extraordinary peace was poured into my body until I was filled to the brim.

I had never experienced anything like it before.

For the next three days, I walked around gloriously intoxicated, not with drugs or alcohol, but with a deep inner calm too wonderful for words.

John and Kelly attended a Baptist church in town, and a week or two later invited me to their home to meet their pastor. Walking into John's lounge carrying my two-month-old son, I had already envisioned the 'man of God' as a rather sombre-looking person aged about eighty-five and wearing a black cassock. I could not have been more wrong.

Kevin, who I guessed was in his late thirties, was not what I expected at all. Unable to contain my surprise, I exclaimed, 'You look *normal!*'

'What do you mean?' he smiled.

'I thought you'd be wearing a long black gown like a priest, not a jumper and jeans! You look more like the man next door!'

The pastor chuckled.

I took to Kevin straight away. He smiled a lot, had a wacky sense of humour and made me feel completely at ease.

Introductions out of the way, I knelt down on the carpet.

Not to confess my sins.

But to change my son's nappy.

CHAPTER THIRTEEN

Playtime

The moment I saw the 'For Sale' sign, I knew our search was over. Our two-bedroom rabbit hutch was not going to accommodate a growing family and the three-bedroom, end-of-terrace house was everything we were looking for. Four rows of houses formed a rectangle with a grassed play area in the centre plus a metal slide, which I knew Lisa would enjoy. Driveways at the rear of the properties meant the enclosed play area was child-friendly, and apart from being popular with the children, parents could keep a watchful eye on them from their kitchen windows at the front of the house.

So, Jonathan and I bought the house, and our family, plus Caesar the dog, moved in.

Standing at the kitchen sink, rubber gloves on and cleaning products in hand, I looked out of the window. Sounds of laughter echoed through the air, beckoning children, 'Come out to play!' Splashes of colour sprinkled the landscape as children of all ages, clad in T-shirts, shorts and dresses had fun with their friends. Some raced along the footpaths while others pedalled frantically on their bicycles, trying to keep up with older siblings. The red metal slide was popular and there was always a queue. Some went down the slide head-first, whooshing so fast they flew straight off the end, their fall broken by the soft grass. Girls played chase around the gardens, darting this way and that so they wouldn't get caught. Boys sprinted around the imaginary Olympic track, followed by shouts of delight as the winner performed his victory circuit along the footpath.

Smiling at the antics, I wondered what Lisa was doing and went into the adjoining dining room to investigate. Our front door was wide open and Lisa was sitting in the doorway, her small frame hunched forward slightly, with both legs over the doorstep. Small for her age, she looked younger than her five years. Gazing intently at the scene before her, Lisa was unaware that I was stood a few feet behind. Her pretty rosebud-pink summer dress didn't match the orthotic red leather boots on her feet. It was like looking at a portrait of a little girl watching the world at play. I wondered what my little angel was thinking as she sat and watched girls her own age playing together.

The scene was brutal. It was the disabled child versus able-bodied children. Despair for the future hurtled through the air and boomeranged with a mighty whack. This was *my* reality. Years of resilience began to crumble, my mind battling to stay in control with a tight rein on my emotions. I couldn't let my daughter see that Mummy was screaming on the inside.

Noticing that my next-door neighbour was on her front lawn, I asked if she could look after Lisa for me, and she was happy to do so. Leaving my daughter safely in her care, I went back inside my house and closed the front door in an attempt to shut the rest of the world out, past, present and future.

Running upstairs to my bedroom I closed the door and sat on the bed, my back leaning against the headboard. A flood-tide of emotions burst their banks and my heart shattered into a million pieces. Loud sobs of intense anguish wracked my body. The image of my precious daughter sat hunched on our doorstep and *so* alone assaulted me with relentless blows. Time after time I had witnessed Lisa being ostracised by her peers because she couldn't join in with them. Suddenly, overwhelmed with it all, I buried my face in my hands and wept.

Utterly exhausted and all cried out, my hands fell onto my lap and my head hung from the heavy weight of sorrow. I felt utterly isolated. Who could I talk to about what it was like to parent a disabled child? Who would wrap me in their arms and comfort me? What about Lisa? Completely drained, not sure if I could go another step, all I could manage was to groan, 'Oh God, help me.'

With my eyes still closed, a brilliant white light appeared at the end of my bed and increased in intensity. Someone was standing there, I just knew it, but was too afraid to open my eyes. Then a voice, full of compassion, spoke directly to my heart. God knew what I was going through and reassured me that I was *not* alone; He would provide the strength I needed to cope, and the grace to endure all things. Secure in His love and enveloped by peace, waves of calm flowed through my body and a healing balm was applied to unseen wounds.

The glorious light slowly faded away and I lingered there a while, soaking in the atmosphere of heaven. Renewed and empowered with courage, I was now ready to face whatever the future held.

Several days later, my daughter was sat on the front doorstep again just as before. A few doors away lived a young girl called Annie, two years older than Lisa. Skipping along the footpath, Annie suddenly turned down our garden path up to our front door, crouched in front of Lisa, and said, 'Hello.' When Lisa didn't respond, Annie looked up at me and without a moment's hesitation enquired, 'Can't she talk?' I explained that Lisa couldn't hear very well, but she could understand some of what was being said through lip-reading. Lisa usually spoke in a soft voice, and although I could understand her, I often had to tell others what she was saying.

Annie looked beyond Lisa's disability and focused on making friends with her.

'Can I come and play with your toys?'

Lisa responded with a nod of her head, and with a big smile, scrambled along the carpet on her hands and knees to fetch her dolls for Annie.

The next day I heard a knock on the front door and was delighted to discover Annie standing there. She asked if Lisa could come out to play. They became good friends and the transformation in our lives was remarkable. Lisa also became popular with some of the other boys and girls, who regularly came to our house to play. It was so heart-warming to see my daughter being included at last!

For Lisa to join the outside games, she needed to become more mobile, and I began to look for a solution; and then Lisa's school provided her with a specially adapted tricycle. Requiring minimum effort to push the pedals, Lisa wouldn't be drained of energy. Having a bike enabled her to participate in races around the play area at the front of our house. Except for one thing – it didn't move very fast. There were other drawbacks too. The tricycle was large, clumsy-looking, and the heavy metal frame made it difficult to manoeuvre. Compared to the other children's bikes it was ugly, and the bright blue paint did little to improve the overall impression. Maybe some stickers would have jazzed it up a bit, but the tricycle belonged to the school so we couldn't customise it in any way. Any attempts to divert people's attention from the fact that it was a tricycle for disabled children would have been fruitless, like trying to disguise an elephant by making it wear a tutu. It just wasn't going to work. So I continued to look elsewhere . . .

My prayers were answered in the form of a bright red go-kart purchased from a nearby store. Lisa was absolutely delighted with her new mode of transport and could peddle it herself with minimum effort. The new hot-wheels were an instant hit around the neighbourhood, especially with the boys. Thanks to the go-kart, my daughter's life was transformed and she was now the centre of attention.

CHAPTER FOURTEEN

Divorced but Not Alone

Three large suitcases stood in a row by the back door. Unable to move or speak, I watched my husband come down the stairs, pick up his bags, and walk away from our ten-year marriage. The sound of the door closing behind him reverberated through my body and soul.

Stricken with panic, I cried, 'God, help me, I can't do this!'

A divine presence filled the room, wrapping me like a reassuring blanket. My life was *not* over. No matter how I felt, whatever the circumstances might yell at me, the truth was clear: I was not alone. A gentle silence permeated the house. 'He will quiet you with His love'.[3] Whatever happened in the future, I knew Jesus would never pack His bags and leave. God's love never walks away.

Now I was faced with a huge dilemma: how to explain to my daughter that Daddy wasn't coming home. Later that afternoon, Lisa's yellow school bus pulled up outside the back-garden fence. I took a deep breath. The driver smiled a cheery 'hello' and I smiled back, concealing the pain within.

Carrying Lisa up the garden path, her two hair bunches bobbed up and down as we walked towards the back door. As far as my little girl was concerned, today was just like any

---

3. Zephaniah 3:17, NKJV.

other day. Routine was important to Lisa; it gave her a sense of security.

Placing my daughter on the sofa, I removed her red winter coat and brightly coloured mittens. Full of enthusiasm, Lisa proceeded to tell me about her day. I didn't want to tell her about mine.

Handing her a plastic mug, Lisa took a few sips of orange juice and devoured a chocolate-cream biscuit. Sliding off the sofa, she crawled across the floor on her hands and knees and then pulled herself onto a child-sized orange plastic chair in front of the television.

At half-past five, Lisa turned her head and looked towards the back door expecting her daddy to walk in. Realising that he wasn't home from work yet, she turned her attention back to the TV.

Ten minutes later, she looked at the door again, but there was still no sign of Daddy. Lisa slid off the chair and crawled over to the sofa where I was sitting. Kneeling in front of me, Lisa gazed intently at my face looking for any tell-tale signs that might provide an answer to the question I had been dreading. 'Where's Daddy?'

Our lives, so intricately woven together, seemed frozen in time. A long silence followed, my heart pierced through and my eyes moistened with tears. Thinking, 'I must be strong for Lisa's sake,' I needed steel in my veins. I had rehearsed this scene already, and as calmly as I could, replied, 'Daddy's not coming home today.'

'Why?'

'Daddy's gone to live in a different house.'

'Who with?'

'His girlfriend.'

Attempting to remain as unemotional as possible – I wanted to spare my five-year-old daughter the same degree of anguish that I felt – I explained that her daddy would not be living with us any more. I will never forget the look on her face.

Had Lisa understood what I had just told her? What was she thinking? How was she feeling? Lifting my daughter onto my lap, I gently wrapped my arms around her and held her close. Jonathan's sudden departure must have come as a big shock to her. Feeling very protective towards my daughter, I didn't want her to get hurt, emotionally or physically, and I tried to shield her heart as best I could. But I knew that she would be affected, one way or another, because when families separate it hurts.

As I broke the news to Lisa, her baby brother was asleep in his cot upstairs. We had celebrated Jamie's first birthday just three months previously. I had no idea how Jamie would be affected by Jonathan's departure, or what it would be like for him to grow up without his father at home. When would we see Jonathan again? How often would he visit his children? Would he take them to *her* house? Just the thought of *the other woman* spending time with my children was too much to cope with.

When my family heard the news, they were stunned at first, and then they became angry. However, their attitude towards him softened over time.

Throughout our marriage, I endeavoured to be a good wife to Jonathan and didn't mind doing most of the cooking and cleaning around the house, even though we both worked full-time before our daughter was born. Jonathan was a good father to Lisa and spent quality time with her every week. If she saw her daddy lying on the carpet, she made a beeline for him and crawled all over his back, giggling as she did so. When out for a walk together, Lisa enjoyed sitting astride Jonathan's shoulders.

While Jonathan lived with us, he never failed to provide for his family. He even tried his hand at various DIY projects around the home, with some amusing results. The thick carpet in the lounge made it difficult to open the door, so Jonathan took the door off its hinges and sawed an inch off the bottom. A while later, dripping with sweat from the exertion of using a handsaw, Jonathan realised that he had sawn an inch off the top of the door instead of the bottom!

My husband was popular, never short of friends, and always willing to lend a hand to people in need. As far as I was concerned, Jonathan and I seemed to get on well and barely rowed about anything. If I did happen to disagree with Jonathan, I tended to keep it to myself because I didn't like confrontation.

However, when Lisa was first diagnosed I felt this was the start of an emotional distancing between my husband and me – one that seemed to grow wider as the months went by. Generally, men like to fix things but Lisa's condition was something that her daddy would never be able to fix.

Jonathan withheld from broaching the subject of our daughter's life-limiting condition because he didn't want to upset me, but I wish we had talked openly about our feelings, because there was no denying that it affected us both. We needed someone to tell us that it was OK to be angry. We needed to speak to someone outside of our situation who was not as emotionally involved as we were – someone to listen, someone to care. Jonathan and I had no idea where to turn to for help, advice or counselling. With far too much on my plate already, I lacked the wherewithal to find a trained professional who could help us through our circumstances. If there were resources available, no one told us about them.

Life had suddenly taken on a whole new meaning for me and my husband. It was certainly not the future we had envisaged together! It was like falling out of a plane and landing in a foreign country where we knew neither the language nor the culture, and without a road map we hadn't a clue where we were going or how to get there.

Did Jonathan and I express our emotions to each other? No, not really. We dealt with our situation the best way we knew how, retreating into our own separate corners and fighting our personal battles in isolation. When Lisa was first diagnosed, what we really needed as a family was someone to hand us a 'Support and Information Fact-Pack'. It would have been beneficial to point us in the right direction and show us where to go for information, advice and support – with names and contact details of any support groups or networks already operating in our area. Such a resource would mean that parents would not be left completely in the dark when trying to discover who they could approach for help with their family's practical, emotional, physical and spiritual needs.

When our second child was born, I hoped that Jonathan and I would be drawn closer to one another, and as a family too. Sadly, that wasn't the case. The hairline cracks in our marriage continued to expand. My life seemed to revolve around caring for Lisa and meeting her needs: round-the-clock care, hospital appointments, plus tests, tests and more tests. Jonathan rarely accompanied us. For whatever reason, I seemed to be the one who sat with Lisa time and time again in a hospital's outpatients' department receiving the latest reports about our daughter's condition.

Maybe we should have spent more time together as a couple and arranged for a babysitter to stay at home with the children while the two of us went out for dinner or a movie, at least once a month, for some respite. The stormy seas of ongoing trials continued to pound against our marriage. Our commitment towards one another was eroding fast, any glimmer of hope beginning to fade. Something *had* to change.

Church had become my lifeline, and I loved every minute of it. God had filled an enormous vacuum in my life, and for the first time in a very long time I experienced a sense of hope rising inside me. Everything was all so new and exciting. The words in the Bible sprang to life and I devoured Scripture with an insatiable appetite. Apart from going to church on Sundays, I attended a home group once a week, plus the occasional prayer meeting. It felt so good to meet with people and have a positive focus – a complete contrast from being left at home with the children most of the time. Thankfully, Jonathan was willing to stay at home and look after our children for one evening a week while I attended various meetings.

On Sundays, the children came to church with me. Lisa really enjoyed Sunday school and I lived in the hope that one day we could all to go to church together as a family – Jonathan did come to my baptismal service.

Most of my time and energy was taken up in caring for Lisa. Having a child with multiple special needs was physically and emotionally draining. Looking back, I can understand how Jonathan might have felt neglected, abandoned even, while I poured myself into caring for our daughter and baby son. Usually by the time I went to bed at night I was so worn out that the moment my head touched the pillow I would be fast asleep within a few minutes.

From the day of our separation I tried to live one day at a time and not worry about tomorrow. It was easier said than done. Not only did I have to fill the roles of both mother *and* father to my children, I was also confronted with the reality of having to manage without Jonathan's wage every month. Scenarios of 'what if' buzzed around my head like flies. Whatever happened, I resolved never to speak ill of Jonathan to his children.

I hoped that Jonathan and I would somehow find a way to be reconciled, but the months came and went with little contact. The day came when I felt I had no choice but to instigate divorce proceedings.

An overwhelming sense of rejection battered my self-worth to a pulp. Over the next few months the weight fell off me, and I went from a dress size 14 down to a size 10. My friends became so concerned at the sight of my pale, gaunt face and thin body, they urged me to see my GP. Apparently, the stress of my ongoing divorce proceedings had increased the level of adrenaline in my body, resulting in a faster metabolic rate and weight loss.

As I was getting ready to go to church one morning, I felt the Lord say, 'I want you to cry today.' Absolutely horrified, I responded with a resolute, 'No way! I'm not crying in front of all those people!' He explained that if I never let people see me cry, they would assume that I was coping and didn't need any help. That morning, for the very first time, I let my guard down in public and allowed people to see what was really going on inside me. I wept through most of the service.

I continued to lean on God and I leaned hard. I'm convinced that I would not have made it without Him. Even with His enabling and support, I still went through patches when I felt so overwhelmed it was unbearable.

A year after Jonathan left home, I received a document through the post stating that our divorce decree was now absolute. I was divorced. The moment I read the document something inside me died.

Recovery takes time. My heart was grieved and my soul harpooned by jabs of anger, resentment, jealousy, grief, regret and sorrow. It never made sense, but there are two sides to every story and I guess Jonathan had his reasons for leaving.

Harbouring bitterness or resentment towards another person does more harm than good. Why prolong the agony? Unforgiveness is like picking at a scab and not allowing the wound to heal.

It was time to let go.

I handed my destructive emotions, thoughts and words to God in prayer and I asked God to forgive my wrongdoings.

The burdens began to lift.

By the grace of God, I was able to forgive Jonathan and his new partner and accept what I could not change.

As the months went by, I discovered that it didn't hurt so much any more.

Truly, forgiveness is one of the most liberating forces on the earth.

CHAPTER FIFTEEN

A Roller Coaster Relationship

I managed to keep all my plates spinning, but only just. Apart from going to church on Sundays, my children and I rarely went out together. Just the thought of taking a disabled child and a toddler into a strange environment was more than I could manage, so I decided that it was much easier to look after them at home instead. My friend took her children here, there and everywhere on a regular basis, which made me feel guilty because my children were missing out on so much. Our family expedition consisted of little more than a short walk to the local shops and back, just once or twice a week. A divorced single mother of two, any prospect of my having a social life vanished into thin air like the vapour trail of a plane. Desperately in need of another adult to talk to, I lived in hope that someone would visit me at home, but no one came and the months passed by.

One day, on discovering that my car wouldn't start, I telephoned a friend and asked if her husband, Gary, could take a look at it for me. I knew how to check the engine oil and coolant levels, top up the screen washer and inflate the tyres, but apart from that I was clueless. Gary arrived the next day accompanied by his brother-in-law, Derek. After fixing the car they stayed for a cup of tea. When Derek went to use the upstairs toilet, he returned with a sheepish grin on his face saying that he was sorry, but he had broken my loo! He offered to come back the next day to fix it.

As promised, Derek returned the following afternoon, and tools in hand, went to fix the toilet. Twenty minutes later, it was done. An adept storyteller, Derek painted vivid pictures of his escapades. He made me laugh too. The conversation flowed well into the evening, and glancing at my watch, I was shocked to discover that it was two o'clock in the morning! We said our farewells and I retired to bed, wondering if I would ever see him again, and hoping that I would. Derek made me feel safe.

Derek became a regular visitor – a welcome break from the isolation and loneliness I felt after my divorce. When I felt the time was right, I introduced Derek to my children, and fortunately they all seemed to get on well. The children enjoyed being taken out for the day, including trips to the coast, play parks and the zoo. This new lease of life was infinitely better than being stuck at home on my own, day after day. With my new set of wings, I was able to regain the confidence to fly again and slowly but surely, began to explore new horizons. But cracks began to appear in the relationship.

I should have paid more attention to the early warning signs, but I didn't, and soon became trapped in the whirlpool of a controlling and verbally abusive relationship. Believing that if I loved him enough then things would improve, I kept going for as long as I could. Every time the relationship ended, Derek would become sweet again and I would take him back. Lonely and bereft after my divorce from Jonathan, I was looking for love in all the wrong places.

My fear of rejection played an integral part in leading me down a path I didn't want to go. In my heart I knew that being a single Christian meant abstaining from sex outside of marriage . . . but I couldn't say 'no'. Derek wasn't a Christian, and I was fighting an inner battle I could not win.

One day in absolute desperation I cried out to God to set me free, once and for all. My prayer was answered and the chains were broken. I told Derek that our relationship was over and this time I didn't take him back again.

Three weeks later, I discovered that I was pregnant.

At this stage, I didn't have a car and so began to attend a church within walking distance. A few months later the pastor informed me that members of his congregation had expressed their desire to help my family. The list included help with the laundry, mowing the lawn, childminding and shopping. This kind gesture took me completely by surprise! Did I take them up on their offer? No, I didn't. I was so used to doing everything myself that I just carried on regardless. Just the thought of asking for help with my daily chores made me feel awkward, and I couldn't possibly hand our dirty laundry over to someone else. It just didn't seem right.

My third baby was born by Caesarean section and I named him Luke. A single mother, I was now faced with the prospect of looking after a newborn baby, Jamie who was almost three, and Lisa, aged seven.

After four months of nonstop parenting while recovering from a major operation, I eventually reached the point of exhaustion, and one afternoon collapsed in a heap on the dining room floor. Too weak to move a muscle, completely devoid of energy, I knew I couldn't remain on the floor because I had children to look after. It was definitely time for a 'break-glass-in-emergency' prayer. 'Lord, please help me,' I groaned. 'I need your strength!' He immediately responded, infusing my body with renewed vigour. Rising to my feet, I simply carried on as before. Had I learned my lesson? Was I now willing to accept the help offered to me by others? No. I just couldn't ask anyone for help.

Apart from my depleted physical state, I was still suffering from the aftermath of the relationship with my baby's father and felt emotionally shipwrecked. One morning, I experienced something unnerving – the lounge walls seemed to be caving in towards me, and then collapsing like a pack of cards! Concerned that I might be heading for a nervous breakdown I telephoned my mother, who invited me and the children to spend a week in her seaside bungalow. For the next five days, I did little else but sleep, while my mother and her husband looked after the children for me. Realising that I couldn't cope at home without back-up, I contacted my pastor, who set the wheels in motion.

CHAPTER SIXTEEN

Not Dying

Nothing can prepare a mother's heart to watch her child slowly deteriorate. No medication can relieve the pain lodged deep within the soul, and no amount of consolation will make it disappear. There was nowhere to run and nowhere to hide. All I could do was be the best mother I could to the sweetest daughter.

By the age of seven, Lisa had decreased mobility in her hands and wrists. Apart from her hands developing into a claw shape, she had lost the ability to straighten her fingers voluntarily and could no longer perform a pincer movement (touching the tip of the thumb with the tip of the index finger). Her grip had become weaker and she could not flex or extend her hands at the wrist.

The prognosis delivered by the paediatric consultant at the children's unit six years ago that Lisa would gradually waste away was unfolding before my eyes. It was clear that Lisa's muscle wasting, which began in her hands and feet, was spreading up her limbs. Both legs had become noticeably thinner below the knee, and her entire leg resembled an inverted champagne bottle. She was also flat-footed.

Visits to the London hospital continued every six months. Having to face up to, and deal with, new medical terms which I had never heard before was all part of the journey. Keeping a cool head during our hospital visits was essential, bearing in mind that my daughter was beside me most of the time. My tears would have to come later, and in the privacy of my own home.

One of the muscle clinic doctors informed me that Lisa's symptoms were consistent with a condition known as peroneal muscular atrophy (PMA), also referred to as Charcot-Marie-Tooth disease (CMT). This hereditary motor and sensory neuropathy causes foot drop, wasting of muscle tissue in the lower legs, weakness in the hands and loss of sensation in the feet. There was no cure. That being said, my daughter presented the muscle team with a puzzle – the onset of CMT usually occurs later in childhood or early adulthood, whereas Lisa had been born with the condition.

Questions continued to haunt me: 'Was I solely to blame for my daughter's debilitating disease?' During the first three months of my pregnancy I took a multivitamin tablet each day to ensure that my baby received the nutrients necessary to grow strong and healthy. Was taking this supplement in any way responsible for Lisa's nerve damage before she was born? I still don't know the answer to that question.

Apart from my wavering emotions, I also had to consider Lisa's feelings during each hospital appointment. Exactly how much she could understand was difficult to ascertain. She didn't ask lots of questions, which was a relief because I wasn't sure how to answer them. Lisa was good at 'reading faces' and I made sure not to appear too anxious or afraid, regardless of how I was really feeling.

As the months went by Lisa became thinner and weaker. This *thing* which ravaged her body seemed unstoppable. I wanted to rescue my child from a future of disability. I wanted to set her free from spending her life, however short, trapped in a body which refused to function normally.

A London doctor took me completely by surprise when he informed me that peroneal muscular atrophy did *not* affect the vital organs! Making sure that Lisa was not within earshot, I replied, 'Are you telling me that Lisa isn't dying?' The doctor confirmed the diagnosis. Lisa's condition was not fatal.

I was stunned! I didn't know whether to allow myself to believe it or not, even though I wanted to.

Dare I hope?

That afternoon as I drove home along the motorway, my mind echoed with: 'Lisa's not dying . . . Lisa's not dying.' I didn't know whether to laugh or cry. In just one moment, it felt like our world had gone from upside down to the right way up. Telling friends and family that Lisa was not dying brought an enormous sense of relief and gladness to one and all.

It was marvellous.

But it didn't last.

CHAPTER SEVENTEEN

She Can't Hear You!

After a preliminary test in London, the muscle clinic doctors had stated that in their opinion Lisa's auditory nerve would not be affected by her condition. However, it soon became apparent that my daughter was not conforming to medical textbooks, and a subsequent hearing test confirmed my fears. Not only was my child disabled, she was losing her hearing as well! Sucked into the vortex of unfamiliar territory, I went round and round in circles. The feat of organising our daily lives amidst a continual maelstrom of ever-changing tides took every ounce of my stamina. Each time I had some direction in my life, another element would be thrown into the mix and the horizon would change again. This threw me for a while, until I was able to regain my equilibrium and focus on keeping my head above water while supporting my family and keeping us afloat. My relationship with God was the life raft I clung on to through stormy seas. I would have gone under 1,000 times without it.

When Lisa's hearing loss was officially diagnosed, I had no idea what to do next. Completely ignorant of deaf culture, it was like trying to find my way to 'I-don't-know-where' with a blindfold on.

Maybe the town library could help? Standing amidst rows of books about hearing impairment and deaf culture, I felt so out of my depth that I just turned around and walked away, sadly none the wiser.

However, help was on the way, and from a totally unexpected source.

Through the grapevine, I heard that an old school friend of mine had become a qualified teacher of the deaf. Christy and I had lost touch with each other over the years and I had no idea where she was. Turning to God in prayer, I said, 'Lord, I need to find Christy. Please help me.'

Two weeks later I was driving through a neighbouring town and remembered that I needed to buy some milk. As I stood in the queue, I realised the lady in front of me looked familiar. It was none other than Christy's mother! Contact details in hand, I couldn't wait to get home and call my old school friend.

It was lovely to hear Christy's voice, and we certainly had a lot of catching up to do. Christy paid us a home visit and came well-prepared, with various items of equipment to test my child's hearing and monitor her responses. Lisa took to Christy straight away, and had great fun singing into a microphone and wearing a set of headphones. For the first time since Lisa was diagnosed with a hearing loss, I was given some valuable insight and practical advice. As a teacher of the deaf, Christy was able to point me in the right direction regarding what was available for hearing-impaired children within the education system. I was astonished to discover that my daughter was entitled to a signing interpreter at school to translate the lessons into sign language, and to help facilitate social interaction during playtime.

Lisa was referred to the audiology department at our local hospital to be supplied with hearing aids. Her first set of hearing aids were standard NHS issue, powered by a small circular battery. If the mould wasn't fitting snugly inside her outer ear, the hearing aid emitted a high-pitched whistling sound. Lisa didn't seem to mind wearing her hearing aids and I'm sure they made a difference, but to what degree I couldn't say.

One day, teachers at Lisa's school informed me that she had 'moderate learning difficulties'. Surely Lisa's academic progress had been hampered because she couldn't hear properly? I first voiced my concerns when Lisa was three years of age in the school nursery, and it had taken four years before she received her first set of hearing aids!

If Lisa couldn't make sense of what was being said at school, then how could she respond to the staff or interact with her peers? In Lisa's case, the school's use of Makaton sign language had initially proved useful but she now required a broader range of vocabulary. The muscle weakness in her wrists and hands also made it difficult for her to write legibly. How frustrating it must have been for her at times!

A few years later my daughter was referred to a hospital's audiology department out of county. The journey took more than an hour by car but proved well worth the trip. When we arrived, an audiologist led us into a soundproofed room and explained that Lisa would undergo a 'pure tone audiometry test' on each ear. A series of sounds varying in loudness (intensity) and speeds of sound wave vibrations (tone) would be played through a set of headphones. When Lisa heard a sound, she had to press a button on the table in front of her. Explaining the procedure to Lisa in simple terms, I then sat a short distance behind her to prevent any distractions.

The test commenced. Precise measurements were taken using an audiometer and the results portrayed in graph form. Compared to the equipment in our local hospital, this facility was leaps and bounds ahead.

Along one wall of the soundproofed room was a panel of one-way glass, and sitting on the other side a technician was operating various knobs and dials on a control panel which resembled the equipment used by a recording studio.

After years spent waiting and wondering, the audiology team were able to provide me with concise information regarding my daughter. Lisa had a sensorineural hearing loss resulting from damage to the auditory nerve between her inner ear and brain. The audiologist explained the hearing process. My daughter's hearing loss was classified as 'moderate-to-severe'. I now had a much clearer idea of what my daughter could and could not hear.

Up to that point, the hearing aids worn by Lisa were very basic with just one setting, a volume control which amplified *all* sound. Lisa was now presented with brand-new state-of-the-art hearing aids, configured to select which sounds and tones needed to be amplified, using data provided by the audiometric results. The aids were very expensive and I was grateful that I didn't have to pay for them. That being said, I still didn't know what the world sounded like to my daughter. Thankfully, she was quite proficient at lip-reading.

Armed with a much clearer understanding of Lisa's hearing loss, I enrolled on a college course to learn British Sign Language (BSL), to be taught how to communicate beyond the rudimentary Makaton signs for 'food, drink, hot, cold and toilet'. Over the next few months, my brain ached so much after signing class that it felt like my head had just completed a marathon! Thankfully, my grey-and-white matter slowly began to get used to the mental aerobics and didn't seem to hurt quite as much. Homework was mandatory, practising the signs learned in class and trying to memorise new ones. Somehow, I found it easier to sign, rather than interpret what the other person was communicating to me. Nevertheless, I passed the final exam and obtained a CACDP British Sign Language Level 1 certificate.

With so much to learn about hearing impairment, I wasn't quite sure where to start. As Lisa grew older, I began to realise more and more what we were missing. Spending quality time just chatting with my daughter, as other mums do, was something I would never get to experience. The progressive muscle wasting in Lisa's hands prevented her from signing adequately, but she could still move her arms and devised a series of movements, based loosely on sign language, which helped her express what she was trying to say.

During the first few years of her life, my daughter communicated using a normal voice. But as she grew older, the progressive muscle weakness caused Lisa's voice to slowly fade away until it was barely a whisper. Unable to tell me exactly what she wanted or how she was feeling wasn't easy for either of us. Sometimes I managed to get the gist of what she meant, and more often than not, could sense when something was wrong.

Over time it became apparent that Lisa was quite bright, and on occasion seemed particularly interested in world events. One day, Lisa and I were watching an interview with Palestinian political leader Yasser Arafat on the news. Turning to me, Lisa signed, 'Who's that?' How could I even begin to explain the political situation in the Middle East using basic sign language?

Family gatherings at birthdays and Christmas tended to pull at my heart strings. Each time my daughter was greeted with, 'Hi, Lisa, how are you?' the conversation would usually end there. My family never learned to sign, although I did show them some key words. Lisa spent most of the time sat in her wheelchair watching from the sidelines, while her cousins played games on the floor. Lisa's muscle weakness often prevented her from playing an active role. Unable to chat with other members of the family, I endeavoured to interpret for Lisa as best I could.

The isolation she endured, year in and year out, was difficult for me to watch. I often wondered what she was thinking, or what it felt like to be Lisa at these times. Sitting at the dinner table pulling Christmas Crackers, everyone laughed at the silly jokes, except Lisa, who sat in silence. She probably wouldn't have understood the humour anyway.

Despite her hearing loss, Lisa developed a close bond with her immediate family, especially her younger brother, Jamie. The fact that they couldn't communicate on a deep and meaningful level was never a barrier in their relationship.

Love has many expressions.

CHAPTER EIGHTEEN

One Mother to Another

One afternoon, Lisa was sat on the toilet when the phone rang. Expecting an important call, I assumed it would only take a few minutes and ran downstairs to answer the phone, leaving Lisa on the toilet. With a handrail on her left to lean on, and the bath on her right, she was able to sit upright on the toilet without any assistance. While speaking on the phone downstairs, I could hear Lisa happily singing away.

A few moments later there was a loud 'thud' on the bathroom floor, followed by silence. Without a moment's hesitation I told the caller, 'I've got to go!' and sped upstairs. My daughter was lying on the floor next to the bath. I can only assume that while singing, she had lifted both arms up in the air to sign the words and, in her exuberance, had lost her balance and fallen off the toilet.

After checking that none of her limbs were injured, I carefully picked my daughter up off the floor, carried her downstairs, and lay her gently on the sofa. About ten minutes later she seemed perturbed and signed, 'Can't see!' I assumed that her vision was blurred due to concussion; she most probably hit her head on the side of the bath or banged it on the floor when she fell.

Twenty minutes later we were in the A&E department of our local hospital, waiting to be seen by the doctor. Lisa's face was very pale. Then her complexion took on a slightly green tinge. She then became ashen-grey and indicated 'Me, vomit!' At that precise moment, a nurse walked past.

'Is she all right?'

'She banged her head and feels sick.'

The nurse handed me a disposable vomit bowl for Lisa, ushered us into a cubicle, and drew the curtains around us. Lisa was placed upon a trolley, the head-end raised, and side supports locked into position. When her body became limp, I knew that we needed some back-up fast.

The nurse came in to take Lisa's blood pressure and I grabbed the opportunity, asking if she could stay with my daughter for a few minutes while I made a quick telephone call. Assuring Lisa that I would only be gone a few minutes, I hurried to the public telephone in a corridor just outside. That morning some people from church were gathering for a prayer meeting, and after a quick explanation I asked them to pray for Lisa, and then rushed back to her.

A doctor entered the cubicle, ascertained the facts, gave Lisa a physical examination, and reported, 'It looks like concussion. We'll need to admit Lisa for observation. Can you stay overnight?'

I had brought an overnight bag with me, just in case, so I sat in the cubicle with my child, the curtains drawn closed. I felt shielded from the outside world, as if it were a sanctuary. My angel, slumped against the pillows, remained ashen-faced.

The next moment, the atmosphere in the cubicle began to change, a tangible peace flooding the room. God had heard our prayers. All of a sudden, Lisa sat bolt upright. Her face beaming with a huge smile and her cheeks now a healthy-looking pink, she looked absolutely radiant! My precious daughter, who just moments before was limp and grey, was now on all-fours, bouncing up and down on the hospital trolley, laughing and singing! Lisa had been miraculously healed of concussion, right before my eyes.

'Now what are we going to do?' I wondered. Regardless of the fact that Lisa had already been admitted and was now fully recovered, I had a strong sense that we were meant to stay in hospital overnight.

Lisa was relocated to the children's ward, and when she was settled into bed, I telephoned the prayer group to thank them for their prayers and announced the wonderful news that Lisa had been healed of concussion. Needless to say, there was great rejoicing.

Having been engrossed with felt pens and a colouring book for half an hour, Lisa decided to take a nap. In need of a short break myself, I went into the corridor in search of a quiet place to sit, pondering why Lisa and I were on the ward that particular evening. Since Lisa's initial diagnosis over five years ago, I had come to recognise divine appointments when someone was in need of special care during one of our hospital visits. I asked the Lord who He wanted me to talk to, and then I saw her.

Down the corridor a few feet away stood a lady I had known previously. Angela was clearly troubled, her back leaning against the wall as if for support. I began to walk slowly towards her.

'Hello, what are *you* doing here?' enquired Angela, surprised to see me.

'Lisa's been admitted overnight. She banged her head but she seems OK now.'

I asked how she was doing. Fighting back the tears, Angela replied, 'My daughter's in again. She needs *another* operation to remove a tumour from her stomach.'

I was lost for words. What do you say to the mother of an eight-year-old child who has cancer? Angela quickly turned her attention back to me and enquired, 'How's the family? How are you coping with Lisa?'

'It's not easy,' I responded. 'But my faith helps. I cry out to God and He gets me through it.'

Angela replied, 'I was raised a Catholic. I took my children to church every week. I used to believe in God . . . so where is He now?' Clearly distressed, and with good reason too, she fought to control her emotions. Taking a few deep breaths, she said vehemently, 'Do you know what my daughter has been through? Six operations. And now she needs *another* one!'

My heart went out to her. When Angela's daughter became ill, she was so angry with God for allowing her child to suffer that she stopped going to church, and turned her back on God. I realised I needed to be gentle with this fearful and fragile mother. The last thing Angela needed was a list of scriptures quoted at her, or a sermon. I treated her in the same way that I would want to be treated in that situation.

'Have you told God how you feel?' I asked, treading carefully.

'No, I haven't. I *hate* Him!'

'Why don't you talk to Him?'

'Why should I?'

'Because He knows how much you're hurting and He wants to help you.'

Angela looked taken aback. 'Yeah, right! I thought I had to be good to talk to Him; be all religious and nice.'

I responded, 'Why not tell Him how you *really* feel?'

Angela didn't realise that she could go to God, just as she was, and tell Him how angry she was with Him. No one had ever told her that she could pour out her heart and just 'tell it like it is', and this was all she needed to hear.

It makes no difference whether you come to God shouting, swearing, screaming, or crying, He won't turn His back on you. You can't shock God. He already knows everything about you.

CHAPTER NINETEEN

Marred Clay Pot

My youngest son was four years of age when his father reappeared. It seemed that Derek was a changed man. Wondering what had happened to make him change his ways, I guarded my heart until I was sure it was safe to proceed.

Derek soon became involved in church life. One day I was surprised to see him on top of the church roof trying to fix it so it wouldn't leak. Derek was welcomed as a helper in Sunday school and seemed to enjoy being with the children. His charismatic personality made him popular with almost everyone.

Turning to church leaders for wise council, I asked if they thought Derek and I had a future together. One advised me not to be too hasty, while another seemed to think Derek and I were right for each other.

Seeking clear direction from the Lord, I came across the following Bible verse: 'Pursue [this] love [with eagerness, make it your goal]'.[4] Believing God was giving me the 'go ahead', I began to consider the implications. Surely it would be better for the children to have a father figure in their lives? Not wanting to repeat past mistakes, I set a very clear boundary regarding our physical relationship; no sex before marriage.

---

4. 1 Corinthians 14:1, Amplified Bible.

Some might consider that rather odd, considering we already had a child, but I wanted to do it right this time.

With no sign of the verbal abuse I was subjected to before, I became convinced that Derek really had changed. Soon we were at the registry office setting a date to become husband and wife.

For our wedding present, friends had paid for Derek and me to spend the night in a lovely mock-Tudor hotel, with a grand four-poster bed. But our wedding night left me with emotional scars that would take many years to heal.

When Derek and I returned to my house, the verbal abuse started as soon as the front door was closed. He never hit me, so I didn't have any bruises on my body. My injuries were internal.

It didn't take me long to realise that 'Pursue [this] love [with eagerness, make it your goal]' was *not* a green light for me to build a relationship with Derek, but referred to God's love. I had taken the words entirely out of context. It was a huge error on my part and I took full responsibility for my actions. No one else was to blame for the choices I made.

It was happening all over again. I was beginning to shut down on the inside. It felt like my soul was dying. I had no choice but to leave home. When Derek was out for the day, I hastily packed some things for myself and the children and went to stay with a friend.

About a week later Derek was offered a job overseas. Other things came to light that assured me that the relationship was over. So Derek and I divorced. We had only been married four months.

It was like being sucked into an aircraft engine and spat out the other side. Only God knows how I managed to keep it all together, which I endeavoured to do for the children's sake.

Being a single Christian woman with a 'divorced' label was hard enough, but the religious stigma of being divorced *twice* was much worse. Shame and guilt reared its ugly head and taunted me with condemnation over and over again.

God 'hates divorce';[5] He sees the anguish of men and women who have suffered rejection and heartache, and children caught in the crossfire. But God can heal the broken-hearted and bind up their wounds.[6]

You can't move forward looking backwards so I handed God the marred clay pot of my battered self-worth. I surrendered to the potter's wheel and slowly but surely was fashioned into a vessel fit for purpose.[7]

It took a while, though.

---

5. Malachi 2:16, NKJV.
6. See Psalm 147:3.
7. See Jeremiah 18:4.

CHAPTER TWENTY

Single Parent Family

It was time for my family to relocate. The housing market was in a slump and the town we lived in wasn't popular, so finding a buyer for my house would require nothing short of a miracle. Coincidentally, my father was getting remarried again and his fiancée, Linda, had just put her three-bedroom house on the market. The size and location of her property was ideal and perfectly suited to my family's needs. Within a month of putting my house on the market, Linda's son, who had recently become an estate agent, procured a buyer.

Situated in a quiet residential street, with the town centre just a seven-minute walk away, our new home was an absolute Godsend. Access to the motorway was a few miles down the road, which made regular visits to the London hospital much easier. My son's lower school was just a few minutes' walk away, and our GP surgery was next door to the school. When the boys transferred to middle school, all they had to do was cross the road.

Living without a partner meant I continued to take Lisa to her hospital appointments on my own, which included routine check-ups throughout the year at our local hospital, bi-annual visits to the muscle clinic in London, regular visits to the audiology department in a different county, plus annual appointments in yet another hospital whose paediatric consultant was interested in Lisa's case. I would have appreciated having someone accompany me for support.

Being a single mother of three children, one of them disabled, had proved a steep learning curve. On the days when I didn't feel well, or had come down with a virus, I did not have the luxury of staying in bed for a few days while my partner got our young children ready for school in the mornings, or put them to bed at night. Thankfully, the older the boys became, the more they could do for themselves. As for Lisa, I had to do almost everything for her. Stricken with a heavy bout of flu one day, everything ached, and I felt totally drained of energy. Seven-year-old Jamie came and sat beside me.

'What's wrong, Mummy?' he asked, concerned.

'It's just a bit of a cold, that's all. I'll be all right,' I replied, blowing my bunged-up nose for the umpteenth time.

Without a moment's hesitation, Jamie put his arm around my shoulder and prayed, 'Please, Jesus, make Mummy better,' followed by a confident, 'He will!'

Moments later his prayer was answered and I was instantly healed.

Knowing that I could turn to God at any time, day or night, kept me from imploding. There was one day when I felt so overloaded, I thought I would burst at any minute. Turning my anger towards God, I swore as I exclaimed, 'You could do this job with Your hands tied behind Your back! But I'm human and I can't do this.' Did God strike me with a bolt of lightning for swearing at Him? No, He didn't. He saw my frustration, He knew my pain, and He loved me just the same.

I had a reclining armchair, given to me by my father, and it became my 'prayer chair'. Every day when I had the house to myself, I would sit in the lounge and pour out my heart to God. By the time I had finished, there was usually a mound of soggy kitchen roll on the carpet next to me. Each and every time, He would pick me up, dust me off, and put me back on my feet again ready for another day.

Apart from my own need to 'vent' from time to time, my children also needed the freedom to express how they were feeling. A firm believer in discipline, I also sensed when to relax the boundaries just a little.

My sons had very different personalities. Jamie was quiet, thoughtful, and patient. Even from an early age, he was no trouble at all, for which I was grateful, because I had my hands full with Lisa. He rarely became cross, except when his younger brother pushed him to the limit. Jamie liked to spend time alone and was quite happy playing with his toys in the bedroom. He liked school, showed respect for his teachers, and rarely got into mischief. He enjoyed playing sports, especially football, and at the age of twelve joined a local football team. Luke had boundless energy, was strong-willed and forthright. Highly creative, his vivid imagination conjured up endless cartoon characters which he skilfully drew from a young age. The accompanying storylines were delightful too. Occasionally a school teacher reprimanded him for drawing cartoons in his book during class. Luke put 'fun' into family!

Fully aware that I could never fulfil a man's role in my children's lives, I prayed that one of the men from church would come alongside my boys, maybe for an hour or so once a month, and teach them 'man stuff'. How would Jamie and Luke understand what it meant to be a husband or a father when they had grown up without a male role model at home? Who would be willing to help and instruct them? I wondered. My heart ached for the boys and I sought an answer to their dilemma. The men at church had their own families to take care of and didn't have time to make room for mine. I struggled with this issue for many years, hoping that one day someone might find the time to come alongside my sons and help them transition from boys to men.

Girls need their daddy too! Lisa would never know what it felt like to have her daddy tell her that she was beautiful or that she was his princess, and then scoop her up in his arms. She would never experience what if felt like for a little girl to climb onto our bed in the mornings and tousle Daddy's hair.

Lisa had her own distinct personality but I would have gained a much clearer picture of her likes and dislikes had she been able to express herself freely and without any constraint. If her legs had worked properly, would Lisa have been sporty? Did she want to write stories? She liked to draw, but trying to grasp a pencil or felt pen with her weak fingers became increasingly difficult. Grasping a thick pen-holder helped a little, but she was unable to draw straight lines and could only produce a wobbly scribble; and her writing was practically illegible. When Lisa was older, the majority of pictures she drew for her family consisted of bright red hearts with 'I love you' scribbled across the page in big letters.

Although my daughter was confident at home, when interacting with strangers or people she was not familiar with, she would seem quite shy until she knew them better. When around her family, Lisa was prone to sudden bursts of energy, which included breaking into joyful song. Lisa enjoyed pulling funny faces too, which made us all laugh. She had a wonderful sense of humour, and she could also be rather cheeky.

When chatting about Lisa's condition with her brothers, I endeavoured to be as honest as I could, depending on their age and how much I felt they could cope with at the time. If I needed to have a good cry, I would lock myself in the toilet, because I didn't want to upset the children.

However, the time came when I decided that it might be better if they *did* see me cry sometimes, and I wanted them to know that they could cry in front of the family too, rather than bottle up their feelings.

We have certainly shed a few tears together over the years.

CHAPTER TWENTY-ONE

Shock Treatment

The hospital room had as much ambience as a cardboard box. A distinct lack of colour on the walls and nothing to provide a welcome distraction, one would never describe the room as child-friendly.

A large box-like structure with knobs and dials on the front and some protruding wires did little to allay my sense of unease. The consultant, Mr Hyde, wasted no time at all and with a nonchalant wave of his hand indicated that I should place Lisa's wheelchair adjacent to the machine. As always, I obliged without question. Did I really have a choice?

'And how is *Lisa* today?' enquired My Hyde, looking straight at me.

Being subjected to the same questions over and over again was nothing out of the ordinary for me, especially when a doctor met Lisa for the first time. As her condition was unique, we were often joined by a plethora of white coats, including students, who more often than not discussed my daughter's case as if we weren't there. I didn't expect doctors to explain *everything* to me, but it would have been nice if they had taken into account that it was my daughter they were talking about and I could hear every word. Fortunately, we did on occasion meet a consultant who included us in the team's dialogue. Their consideration helped take the sting out of the fact that my daughter had an incurable illness.

After consulting with his colleagues, Mr Hyde sat opposite Lisa and declared, 'I want to hook Lisa up to this machine and check her response to electrical stimuli.' I was distinctly uneasy at the thought of my daughter being given electric shocks, but I was on his territory now and felt I had no other choice but to let him go ahead. Hopefully the results would be of some benefit.

The electromyography machine (EMG) sent an electrical charge into the patient's muscle cells – via electrodes attached to the skin – and a graph recorded the level of response.

Sticky pads were placed on Lisa's arms and legs, directly against the skin. A long narrow wire connected each pad to the machine. Mr Hyde turned one of knobs, sending an electrical current along my daughter's limbs. The machine recorded the length of time it took for the current to travel along the nerves from point 'A' to point 'B'.

Initially the voltage was quite low. In a normal response, the level of stimulus would cause the muscles to contract with a 'twitching' movement. But Lisa didn't move at all.

The exercise was repeated using a stronger current, and this time Lisa flinched. I was curious to know what the sensation felt like. The consultant turned the knob again, increasing the voltage even higher. Judging by the distraught expression on Lisa's face, she must have thought, 'What on earth are you doing to me?' Having to witness my daughter being subjected to this procedure was really difficult; I just hoped that one day other children would benefit from all the tests that Lisa so bravely endured.

A few moments later, one of the doctors interjected, 'Let's give Lisa a short rest, shall we?'

I was very grateful to him for calling a halt to the test; for a while, at least. Turning his attention to me, the consultant asked if I would like to have a go. I agreed, albeit reluctantly, if only to show Lisa that I was willing to experience what she had just been through. My arm was hooked up to the monitor and a few volts of electricity sent through the pads, causing my muscles to twitch involuntarily. It felt strange, like nothing I've ever felt before, and rather unpleasant too.

Not satisfied with my daughter's results, Mr Hyde remarked, 'Let's give Lisa one more try.'

Reattaching her to the 'electric-shock machine', he increased the voltage. Lisa was visibly distressed, but there was still no response in her muscles. I wanted to stop Mr Hyde, but felt powerless to act because he was in control. One of the symptoms of Lisa's condition was decreased sensitivity to external stimuli, but even so, I had no way of knowing the degree of pain she had suffered during the test.

As if Lisa had not been through enough already, Mr Hyde turned the voltage up again, and this time to its maximum level. Lisa's whole body jumped, her face contorting with shock and pain, and tears rolled down her cheeks. It took an awful lot to make Lisa cry, and I knew it must have been really painful for her.

Pushed to the limits of my endurance, I simply couldn't bear to watch my daughter suffer any longer. The test results couldn't help Lisa, so what was the point? Silently I cried, 'Lord, please help us; make him stop!' The consultant might not have finished with his tests, but Lisa and I had had more than enough. My maternal instinct to protect my child had reached breaking point, and all I wanted to do was take my daughter and run.

Just as I was about to intervene, a tall man appeared in the doorway and in a very kind voice, asked, 'Can I borrow Lisa?' Framed by the light, he looked like an angel sent from heaven. Mr Hyde agreed, and Lisa and I bid a hasty retreat from what was, in my opinion, more of a torture chamber then a medical room.

Our deliverer took us into another area and introduced himself as Daniel. A specialist in his field, Daniel had been working on a piece of equipment he had invented: a circular hand-held disc, approximately the size of a side plate, connected by wires to another piece of equipment. By simply sweeping the disc just a few inches above Lisa's body, it could register her nerve conduction and transfer the data onto a computer. Unlike the awful test which Lisa had just been subjected to, Daniel's ingenious device was painless.

CHAPTER TWENTY-TWO

The Getaway

I dreamed of faraway places, lost in thought of a remote tropical island with no means of communication with the outside world. Swaying in a hammock suspended between two palm trees on a golden beach, not a soul in sight, was my idea of heaven. Gazing at the turquoise ocean just a stone's throw away, the rhythm of the waves lulled my mind into calm serenity. Relaxing in the shade, a warm summer breeze caressed my senses. From time to time a waiter appeared out of nowhere, bringing me a glass of refreshing fruit cocktail. A few feet away stood a small beach cabin nestled under coconut trees. My own personal chef, whom I never saw, left delicious food on the veranda table and cleared away the dishes afterwards. When I dreamed like this, my vivid imagination provided a brief respite from the twists and turns of life.

Mental relaxation was a form of escape, but what about my body? Lifting and carrying Lisa every day, and raising a very active family, put my slender frame under considerable pressure. If only I could get away for a few days to recharge my batteries. It had been ten years since Lisa's birth and I had not been on holiday. Suffering from exhaustion, so tired that I could barely keep my eyes open, I knew that if I didn't get away soon, I would collapse. But where on earth would I get the money?

One day, out of the blue, my stepfather's son paid me a visit. Seeing the black circles around my eyes, Scott exclaimed, 'You need a holiday. Would you like to go to Malta?'

I could not believe my ears!

Scott had relatives on the island whom he visited on a regular basis. Working for a major airline company for a number of years, Scott was entitled to a staff discount on a 'friends and family' ticket. He insisted on paying for the flights and the hotel. My prayers had been answered.

Desperate to grab the offer of a holiday with both hands, I had to stop and consider the children. Who would look after them? When I told our next-door neighbour about the possibility of my taking a holiday, Abbey didn't hesitate. She and her daughter Holly, who worked as a carer, would look after the children and stay in my house while I was away. Assured that my children would be in very safe hands, I began to make plans for a much-needed break.

Explaining to Lisa and her brothers – aged six and four respectively – that I was going away for a rest and would return in seven days with a nice present for them, they accepted that 'Mummy needs a holiday' and encouraged me to go. They were more than happy to be looked after by Abbey and Holly, whom they knew very well.

A few days later I received a 'fly in the ointment'. After telling a friend about the holiday, she responded that she couldn't understand how I could leave the children for a whole week. Her unexpected response cut me to the quick and I was lost for words. The last thing I needed was a massive guilt trip. I wanted to explain how exhausted I felt, and that if I didn't get away soon I might suffer a complete breakdown, and who would look after the children then?

I was undeterred by my friend's outburst but I also faced a big obstacle: my fear of flying. The closer the holiday came, the more anxious I felt, and urged friends to pray for me.

When the day finally arrived, I put my trust in God and walked across the airport tarmac, climbed the metal steps and boarded the aircraft. Slightly nervous, at least I wasn't screaming my head off. Not yet anyway. The last thing I needed was a panic attack at 30,000 feet.

After a while I began to relax and peered through my window. What an incredible sight! It was the first time I had seen God's creation from so high above. As we flew over the highways and byways, I realised that nothing and no one is hidden from His sight. He knows every person who lives in the dwellings scattered across the vast terrain, even in the remotest valleys. Flying above the sea I was amazed at how tiny the ships appeared as they navigated across the water. For the most part, my first flight had been an enjoyable experience.

As we approached Malta, I was surprised to discover that most of the landscape was cream and beige in colour, and in stark contrast to the green fields of England. After the plane's near-perfect landing, Scott and I collected our luggage and we were soon driving along the streets of Malta in a hired car.

Scott dropped me off at the hotel and then drove to his relatives' house where he was staying for the week. My hotel in St Paul's Bay seemed pleasant enough and the staff were polite and friendly. When it was time for bed, the moment my head hit the pillow I went out like a light and slept soundly for the next twelve hours. It was the best night's sleep I had had in a very long time.

Swapping the cold British winter for a sunny Mediterranean island for a week, and on my birthday, was such a treat. Spending time on my own, completely uninterrupted, was the best medicine in the world. I could eat breakfast in peace and quiet. I was a very happy woman indeed. I did not have to wake up early for Lisa's school bus, had a break from heavy lifting, and there was no need to keep an eye on the clock to fit in with my children's routine.

My holiday in Malta was, without doubt, a healing experience. Malta was more than I could have dreamed. I spent time ambling along side streets, taking in the beauty of the Mediterranean gardens and architecture. I became friendly with some of the others staying in the hotel too. It was as blissful as I had imagined.

Until I was interrupted by the real world.

'Lisa's really ill, she might be dying! She needs an urgent operation; it's a matter of life or death! They need your consent before they can operate.'

I had been awakened by Scott pounding on my door.

Could this be true? After calming Scott down, I asked him to tell me exactly what had happened. Far from home, I felt helpless. Desperate to fly to my daughter's side, I dressed and ran downstairs to the reception desk and asked the night clerk to place an urgent call to the hospital. I was so grateful to be able to get through to the doctor in charge of Lisa's case, and explained my circumstances.

'What's happened? Is Lisa all right?' I asked, desperate for news.

'I can assure you that Lisa is in no danger whatsoever,' replied the doctor, surprised by my distress.

'I've just been told that she might be dying and needs an emergency operation!'

'I don't know who told you that, but let me explain.'

The female doctor informed me that Lisa had developed a minor chest infection and a small amount of mucus had built up in her lungs. Unable to cough up the secretions due to her weakened chest muscles, the doctor had decided that it would be better to admit Lisa for the night and a physiotherapist would help clear her lungs. The doctor also wanted to administer some strong antibiotics to prevent the condition from developing further, for which parental consent was needed. It was standard procedure. Being over 1,300 miles from home, I obviously couldn't sign anything, but the doctor assured me that they could still proceed without my written consent. Desperate to get to Lisa, I told the doctor that I would book the next flight back to the UK, to which she replied, 'There really is no need; Lisa will be fine. You stay where you are and make the most of it. She'll be going home in a few hours anyway.'

Reassured by the doctor that Lisa's condition was not serious, I still wanted to cut my holiday short and rush to my daughter's side. I looked at the clock – it was still very early in the morning and the sun had not come up yet. There was no point in going back to bed because I wouldn't be able to sleep, so I sank down onto a comfortable armchair in the reception area. I wanted to phone Abbey to find out what had happened but it was far too early in the morning to wake her up. I spent the rest of the night churning things over and over in my mind and praying.

My return flight to England was in two days' time. Unable to wait that long I telephoned the airline in the hope they could bring my flight forward so I could leave that day. The airline rep delivered the bad news: 'There's been a freak snowstorm in England. The airports are closed. They're snowbound.' I was well and truly stuck in Malta and there was nothing I could do about it. Feeling totally helpless, I wondered how Lisa must have felt not having her mummy there beside her when she was in hospital.

A couple of days later, my holiday ended. The airport at my destination had cast off its blanket of snow. Boarding the plane, I felt relieved to be returning home at last. As we approached the south coast of England we flew through a glorious sunset, the sea glistened with a myriad of colours, and the White Cliffs of Dover were swathed in pink. As the plane approached the runway to land, I felt a tug on my heart and my eyes filled with tears.

It felt so good to be home and I couldn't wait to see the children. The moment I stepped through the front door, the boys ran straight into my open arms almost knocking me over in their excitement to see me, and eager to tell me their news. Hurrying into the lounge to see my daughter, the moment I laid eyes on her I was shocked. She did not look at all well. She seemed tired, her face pallid and grey. The moment Lisa saw me she broke into a smile. I couldn't get to her fast enough. Lifting her out of the wheelchair, I carried her to the sofa, put her on my lap and gave her a big hug. Choking back the tears, I whispered, 'I'm home now. Everything's going to be all right.'

CHAPTER TWENTY-THREE

When Hope Disappoints

I longed for someone to discover a miracle breakthrough to prevent Lisa's condition from progressing further, but it was not to be. Surely someone, somewhere, would eventually discover both the cause and the cure to benefit not only my daughter but others too. In the meantime, Lisa's muscles became weaker and weaker and lost their bulk and she grew increasingly thinner. The muscle wasting had spread up her limbs, affecting her thighs and upper arms. It was so hard to watch her body being ravaged from the unrelenting genetic disorder. Feelings of helplessness tried to pull me down, but I had to keep going.

Lisa's AFOs had supported her ankles thus far, but when the muscle wasting spread to her thighs the AFOs were no longer sufficient, necessitating another trip to London to see John Canali, our orthotist.

Once again it was time to learn a new word in my special needs vocabulary: the Knee Ankle Foot Orthosis or 'KAFO'. Constructed from plastic and metal, the KAFO went from foot to thigh. A custom-made plastic cuff encompassed the thigh. On either side of the thigh cuff was a strong metal rod which ran down each leg and was attached to the AFO. The metal rods were hinged at the knee. Across the front of the knee was a plastic guard, and a horizontal metal bar over the top. The knee joint could be locked in full extension, making Lisa walk straight-legged because she couldn't bend her knees. Every time Lisa wanted to sit down, she had to grab the horizontal metal bar and pull it upwards to release the hinge joints.

Lisa never complained about having to wear KAFOs. She rarely complained about anything. The calipers were not too bulky so it was easy to pull Lisa's trousers over them.

Would I ever get used to seeing my daughter's legs covered in metal and plastic?

Unable to walk unaided, Lisa used a walking frame called a rollator. It had castors at the front, padded armrests and vertical handgrips. Used mainly at home and school, Lisa occasionally walked outside, but if the terrain was uneven it would topple over; and she couldn't walk far.

Lisa's muscle wasting continued to spread further up her arms and legs and eventually reached her trunk. By the age of ten the gradual loss of muscle function in her torso had become more noticeable. Lisa's spine had developed a sideways curvature (scoliosis) and her lower back curved excessively inwards (lordosis). Her bottom stuck out, and when she lay flat on her back there was a large gap between her lumbar region and the floor. On one of our many trips to London, a muscle clinic doctor informed us that Lisa would need to wear a chest brace to support her spine, otherwise her breathing would be compromised.

Mr Canali measured Lisa's trunk from her armpits to her hips, and arranged for a brace to be made. The thoracolumbosacral orthosis (TLSO) supported Lisa's spine and enabled her to maintain a correct posture when sitting or standing. Made of strong plastic, the rigid chest brace covered the trunk from under the arms to over the pelvis, with an indent at the waist. The vertical front opening was fastened into place using three horizontal Velcro straps. The new plastic jacket fitted snugly around my daughter's thin frame.

Lisa had to wear the brace throughout most of the day, especially when sitting or standing. A thin vest or T-shirt worn underneath helped to prevent skin chafing. Before Lisa had the brace, she used to sit slouched to one side and she now appeared more comfortable positioned upright.

The mobility and function in Lisa's hands, knees and hips continued to decrease, partly due to the contractures. Unable to straighten her legs at the knees or hips, Lisa was booked in for the first of many physiotherapy sessions at the London hospital. Renowned for their skill and expertise, people travelled from all over the world to receive treatment there.

I laid my daughter on a cushioned workbench, flat on her back, and the stretching exercises began. Lisa's legs were permanently bent at the knee. The physiotherapist, clad in a white tunic top and dark-blue trousers, placed her left hand on Lisa's ankle to hold it in place, and with her right hand gently but firmly pushed down on the knee to stretch the muscles and straighten the leg. After holding the leg for a minute or so she let go to give Lisa a break. It was clearly not a pleasant experience. Although I knew the exercises were necessary to help loosen the contractures and therefore aid her mobility, it was hard to see her in discomfort.

Lisa's feet always flopped downwards and she lacked the muscle power to maintain the correct position. On another occasion, the physio took a firm hold of Lisa's ankle and bent her foot upward until 90° to her calf. She didn't stop but continued bending the foot until the angle went past the normal range. Lisa winced. Her expression said it all, and opening her mouth wide, yelled a silent, 'Owww!' I felt powerless to act. All I could do was stand there and watch my daughter suffer, because it was 'for her own good'. Eventually I couldn't bear it any longer and said, 'That's enough.' I was relieved the session was over and I'm sure Lisa was too.

When Lisa had outgrown her major buggy and a wheelchair was provided, she lacked the muscle power to push herself further than a couple of meters on a smooth surface and progress was very slow. The first time I saw my daughter in a wheelchair, a pang of sorrow stabbed my heart.

One day, Mr Canali announced that he had designed some new calipers for children and there was a possibility that Lisa might be able to stand and walk unaided. In due course, measurements were taken for Lisa to be fitted with the new calipers. For the first time in my daughter's life I had *hope*. With the orthotist's expertise, and God's power, I believed that all things were possible[8] and the burden I had carried for so long began to fall away. I didn't want to say too much to Lisa in case it didn't work. She had become used to our regular trips to London, and as far as she was concerned it was just another appointment. I did tell her that we were going to try something new to help her walk.

The big day had arrived and as instructed, Lisa and I went to the physiotherapy department where Mr Canali had arranged to meet us. Eagerly anticipating the life-changing event, friends were praying and my hopes were high. Mr Canali walked into the physio room carrying a gizmo made from plastic, metal, and Velcro straps. Similar in appearance to Lisa's KAFOs, it covered more of the body, with plastic, leather straps and cables to support the pelvis and chest area.

Laying my daughter flat on her back, he proceeded to fit Lisa with the new calipers and brace. The moment of truth had finally arrived. Mr Canali placed Lisa onto her feet and asked me to hold her whilst he checked that everything fitted correctly and to see if any adjustments were needed. The firm plastic brace around Lisa's abdomen made her stand bolt upright. I had not seen her standing that straight for a very long time. Everything seemed to be in order. It was time to let go.

I held my breath and said a silent prayer, 'Please, Lord, let this work.'

Lisa stood for a few seconds and then began to fall forwards. Mr Canali, who was knelt on the floor in front of Lisa, reached

---

8. See Matthew 19:26.

out his hands, held her steady and said, 'Let's give her a moment or two to get used to it.'

He let go and once more, Lisa began to topple.

He was not going to give up easily.

'One more time.'

Lisa began to turn pale and I thought she might faint.

'I think that's enough for now, Lisa,' said Mr Canali. He placed her back on the bench and said, 'Let's take this off now, shall we?' He turned to me. 'I'm sorry to disappoint you, but I don't think this is going to work. Lisa's lumbar muscles aren't strong enough to support her, even with the help of the brace. She won't be able to walk on her own, but at least we tried, that's the main thing.'

I thanked Mr Canali and said goodbye. I wheeled my daughter out of the hospital and drove us home.

I was *so* angry with God.

'What's the point in having faith? What's the point in believing in You, if You aren't going to do anything? Why didn't You help?' The disappointment was overwhelming. In anger and frustration, I said, 'That's the last time I build my hopes up!'

At the London hospital, one of the places where people vented their feelings was the ladies' toilet. On the inside of a cubicle door someone had written a verse from the Bible, no doubt hoping that people would gain comfort from it. However, the choice of expletives which followed indicated that not everyone shared their viewpoint.

Inside another cubicle scribbled on the wall, there seemed to be a running dialogue between two people, about faith. It was very honest. God loves it when we are real with Him!

CHAPTER TWENTY-FOUR

A Truly Special School

Lisa spent seven years at the school for children with special needs. A mixture of discovery and learning, joy and heartache, I never knew what was coming next. On some days, I would be blessed by her achievements, but on other days I would be informed 'she can't do this' or 'she'll never do that' and feel that familiar stab yet again. Technology, splints and educational tools had sought to make the seemingly impossible possible. Amidst the joys were pitfalls; some days were fun-filled and others interspersed with unavoidable accidents and injuries. It was a mixture of 'Well done, Lisa!' and 'What's happened now?' Whenever I received a phone call from the school my heart would sink, because more often than not it meant that something was wrong.

To be greeted with a cheery smile or a kind 'hello' every time I visited the school was a soothing balm to my soul. These children had a way of making me feel accepted and loved. Always giving, they were not consumed with their own personal needs but seemed mindful of others. I felt included in their world. They wanted to make friends with people and didn't mind that we were different because we are able-bodied. Children with special needs possess an innate ability to make outsiders feel like insiders. My eyes had been well and truly opened to the joys and delights of how these children graced the world just by being in it. Their general care and concern towards others left an indelible imprint on my memory that will never be erased. They taught me far more then I could ever teach them. These children changed my life in ways I could never have thought or imagined.

In all the years that Lisa attended the school, invitations to play at another child's house, or go to a birthday party, were rare. With Lisa travelling to and from school on the bus each day, I rarely got to meet other parents and was unaware of any parent support groups.

Lisa seemed to integrate with the other children well. There was never a mention of disruptive behaviour on her part, and she was actually quite quiet. Occasionally when Lisa came home from school she would seem a bit 'off'. She was unable to articulate what was wrong and therefore I was none the wiser. I was grateful to the staff for keeping me informed of any incidents I needed to be aware of. Overall her teachers gave the impression that Lisa was generally well-behaved, one of them even stating that Lisa was a pleasure to have in her class. She seemed to gel with some children more than others. Lisa appeared to be wary of boisterous children, especially those who were excessively loud, or whose arms and legs flailed about, and I can only assume that she felt vulnerable because her muscles were too weak to defend herself.

I really missed not being able to chat with my daughter about her day at school. There was a school-home book which recorded any notable events and therefore I had some idea of how Lisa was getting on and the work she was doing in class. The report book was also useful for informing the teacher of any family news, including how we had spent the weekends and holidays.

When Lisa was nine years old the school arranged a trip to LEGOLAND® in Denmark. Lisa had never flown before and was excited at the prospect. Later that evening the local television news programme aired a brief report about the school's trip, including a segment showing the children and adult helpers beside the steps ready to board the plane. It was a lovely surprise to see my daughter on television and I was glad to hear that a good time was had by all.

It was Lisa's first appearance on television but it would not be her last. A film crew from the BBC arranged a visit to Lisa's school and recorded some footage for their 'Children in Need' appeal.[9] The annual televised event raised public awareness of worthy causes, offered fund-raising ideas, and instructed viewers on how to make donations. Hoping to see my daughter on TV, I spent the entire evening glued to the television screen in the hope of catching a glimpse of her. During the programme, I received a phone call from a very excited friend, telling me, 'I've just seen Lisa on television! She was in the school playground rolling down a grassy slope and laughing. She was having a great time!'

I had missed the clip!

Disappointed, I stayed up for hours hoping the clip would be repeated at some point but when midnight came I didn't think they would show it again, and went to bed. The next day someone informed me that Lisa had been on television again, just ten minutes after I had gone to bed. I was so upset at having missed the chance of seeing my daughter on TV, not once but twice!

Memories of Lisa's schooldays will remain in my heart for as long as it's beating. I owe my deepest gratitude to the staff, including volunteers, who took good care of the children. These children set a precedent for how we should treat our fellow human beings, and they were a hard act to follow.

---

9. Exact year not known.

CHAPTER TWENTY-FIVE

Worth Every Penny

In my quest to find the right secondary school for Lisa, I discovered a school for the deaf in a neighbouring county. It seemed the ideal environment, but could they cope with Lisa's physical disability? There was only one way to find out, so I made an appointment to meet the principal. In need of wisdom and guidance, I began to pray and an image came to mind of a long, curved driveway lined on either side with tall trees, surrounded by beautifully manicured lawns. At the far end stood a grand Victorian-looking house with long sash windows.

The school was nestled in the heart of the countryside and surrounded by parkland. Turning my car off the road, I drove through a large set of double gates and came to an abrupt halt. My mouth fell wide open. In front of me was a long, curved driveway lined with trees and a grand house at the end. It was the same image I had seen when I prayed for guidance. It seemed like confirmation that it was the right place for my daughter and I felt reassured. Filled with peace, I parked the car and made my way to the front entrance.

My first impression of the school was positive. The internal décor was homely, with lots of natural wood including wood panelling on the walls. A member of staff led me to the principal's office and introduced me to Mr Jones. Friendly and approachable, he invited me to take a seat and then offered a brief synopsis of the school. The pupils, aged between eleven and nineteen, had varying degrees of hearing loss, ranging from 'hearing impaired' to 'profoundly deaf'. The national curriculum was taught by teachers of the deaf using BSL and Sign Supported English (SSE) with speech. Some of the pupils had additional physical disabilities, and others, learning difficulties. The school offered residential facilities for boarders to stay during the week from Monday morning to Friday afternoon. Most of the pupils remained at home during half-term and public holidays, but arrangements could be made for children who needed to stay at school over the weekend. The older pupils had their own lounge for socialising, playing games, or watching TV (some of the programmes had subtitles).

Mr Jones informed me that Lisa's current school had already sent him a report outlining her individual needs. I explained that Lisa's muscle weakness in her hands affected her ability to sign, and enquired whether or not she would have a problem communicating with the staff and children. The principal informed me that his staff would develop an 'Individual Action Plan' for Lisa, taking her disability into account, and working towards improving and enhancing her communication skills to interact more fully with the staff and her peers. Lisa would be encouraged to achieve her full potential.

I then asked about Lisa receiving physiotherapy each week to prevent her contractures from worsening. Without regular stretching exercises Lisa's mobility would be compromised, and any loss of independence was detrimental to her self-esteem. I was assured that if a pupil's Statement of Special Educational Needs stipulated the provision of physiotherapy, they would be seen by the peripatetic physiotherapist who visited the school each week.

More questions followed and I was pleased to discover that not only did the school offer a holistic approach towards the pupils' well-being, it was also founded on Christian principles.

A tour of the school followed. The moment we entered the classroom, I was taken aback. It was like entering another world. Lisa's world. Natural light flooded through long sash windows, making the room appear warm and inviting. The walls were a splash of colour, displaying various posters and samples of pupils' work. It was like any other classroom, except the teacher had a transmitter attached to her neck lanyard and the pupils wore hearing aids.

Mr Jones introduced me to the teacher, who offered a warm welcome. One of the girls was speaking, but her diction wasn't clear and I couldn't understand what she was saying. Maybe she was profoundly deaf. Apart from my daughter, this was the first time I had ever heard a deaf child speak. The pupils communicated using a mixture of sign language and speech, some spoke clearer than others, but they all seemed confident and animated. These boys and girls understood what it was like to be a deaf person living in a hearing world, and I felt sure that Lisa would fit in very well indeed.

Exiting the classroom, Mr Jones and I proceeded to the dining room at the far end of the lobby. Everything was bright and clean. One of the cooks had a chat with me about the meals they provided during the week. Lisa had never been a fussy eater and I didn't envisage any problems at school. However, I wasn't sure if she would eat at all to start with, given that she was shy around people she barely knew. Hopefully, Lisa would soon become used to her new environment and grow in confidence as time went on.

In the centre of the hallway was a regal-looking open staircase leading up to the bedrooms on the first floor, and a lift beside the stairs. The boys' bedrooms were at one end of the landing and the girls' rooms the other, and they were not allowed in each other's bedrooms. Each room was shared with at least one other pupil. The bedroom allocated to Lisa was clean and tidy and pleasantly decorated. It had a very homely feel. Lisa could personalise her area of the room, with family photos on the bedside cabinet and posters on the wall. She would be sharing the bedroom with another girl.

This school seemed to tick all the boxes. My daughter had been isolated far too long already and I was confident that she would benefit from this environment, both academically and socially. At long last I had found a group of qualified people who could communicate, empathise, educate, motivate, befriend, comfort, support and assist my daughter. The school seemed all of these things and more.

If Lisa resided in school during the week then I could spend more quality time with my sons. Caring for Lisa took up 80 per cent of my time and there wasn't much energy left over for Jamie and Luke. They deserved better from me, and I knew it. I could never make up for those years and now and then, in the back of my mind, I felt a tinge of guilt.

The time had come to show the school to Lisa. When I explained to Lisa that we were going to visit a school for deaf children she seemed OK with the idea. On that particular day, the principal wasn't there and we were accompanied by a different member of staff. The transformation in Lisa was remarkable. Instead of her usual shyness, it was as if someone had flicked a switch inside her, and she sprang to life. When Lisa was greeted in sign language, with speech, it immediately caught her attention.

When I pushed Lisa's wheelchair into the classroom, her face was an absolute picture! It was the first time she had seen a room filled with children her age wearing hearing aids and signing, and the teacher signed too. Her eyes sparkled as she took it all in. As far as I could tell, Lisa seemed to acknowledge, 'This is my world, these are my people, and I'm one of them.' She had made the connection.

For the first time in a very long while, my daughter could integrate and be understood by those around her. She could learn to chat with girls her own age and approach her teenage years being able to let people know the challenges she faced, using a language they could understand.

The teacher introduced Lisa to the rest of the class, and the girls and boys signed a cheery, 'Hello.' One by one they introduced themselves to Lisa by finger-spelling their name, with speech. Lisa nodded in acknowledgement, already warming to their friendly manner. One of the girls, who seemed a year or two older than Lisa, stood up and came over to her. Signing proficiently, she seemed excited to have Lisa join them. Whether or not my daughter could understand what was being communicated, if her expression was anything to go by, she seemed delighted to be making new friends. Content and deeply gratified, I had discovered some buried treasure that I didn't even know existed.

We entered the dining room and a couple of staff introduced themselves, and with a big smile informed Lisa, 'We're sure you'll like the meals here because we've got a very good cook.' Lisa seemed a bit reserved but I felt confident that she was well on the way to accepting her new environment.

Walking through the foyer, we met the woman responsible for Lisa's pastoral care. She assured my daughter that if she had any questions or concerns, or wasn't feeling well, then she could go to see her. She seemed very kind. It was a relief to know that my daughter was in good hands.

It was time to show Lisa her new bedroom and I wheeled her into the lift. I considered this to be quite a hurdle and wondered how Lisa would react. Would she like it? What if she flatly refused to sleep there? I was about to find out.

Lisa's reaction to the bedroom was positive. She seemed to like the overall appearance of the room, plus the beautiful view from the window. There were large green lawns as far as the eye could see, lots of trees and colourful flowerbeds. I explained to Lisa that she could bring anything she wanted from home to put around her bed.

So far so good.

At that moment Lisa's prospective new roommate, Tamika, walked into the bedroom. A couple of years older than Lisa, she seemed confident and friendly. Not only would Lisa have a friend not that much older than she, it was good for her to share a bedroom rather than be on her own. It was time to ask Lisa the big question, 'Would you like to sleep here?' Without hesitation, Lisa nodded, 'Yes.' I was delighted!

Now I was faced with the task of convincing the education authority to release the funding for a residential placement for Lisa. In my experience, it was easier to push a hippopotamus into a fridge than it was to procure money from the government for a 'statemented' child. Resolute and undaunted, I knew that my child's future was at stake and she was worth every penny!

A meeting was arranged at Lisa's special needs school to discuss her transition from one school to the next, and reach a final decision. Those present at the meeting included Lisa's class teacher, a class assistant, the school physiotherapist, educational psychologist, the chief education officer and me. One by one, each person expressed their opinion regarding whether or not my daughter needed to go to a school for the deaf. I sat quietly and listened, waiting patiently to have my say.

Overall, I got the impression that according to the staff, Lisa didn't need the specialised provision offered by the school for the deaf, and would not benefit a great deal from being there. One member of staff was quite adamant, stating that Lisa's needs were already being met where she was, so why change schools at all? On the whole, the arguments against Lisa relocating far outweighed those in favour. The meeting was not going as I had hoped. I had not expected that much opposition, especially from those who I thought were on our side.

After some time and discussion, the chief education officer came to a decision; the funding would not be provided. I did not say a word. I wasn't annoyed, disappointed, or upset; on the contrary, I felt very calm, believing that God would give me the right words to say at the right time. Turning towards me, the chief education officer said, 'Mrs Nolan, I'm aware that you haven't spoken yet. Is there anything you would like to say?'

As I began to speak, a river of words flowed from my mouth, and in a clear and concise manner I stated the reasons why my daughter should attend the school for the deaf. My comments seemed irrefutable and the wisdom certainly didn't come from me! After presenting my case I leaned back on my chair and waited. The room was so quiet you could have heard a pin drop.

The chief education officer was the first to speak. He looked me straight in the eye. 'You can have the money,' he said. The local education authority (LEA) was going to pay for Lisa to attend a school in another county *and* would also pay for a taxi to take her there and back each week.

A few days later I was confronted with the stark reality that my daughter was going to a residential school. Realising that Lisa would be living away from home from Monday to Friday caused an acute physical reaction: chronic diarrhoea. My GP put the symptoms down to stress. As far as I was aware, I didn't feel anxious about Lisa staying at her new school. But there was no denying the truth; I was suffering from a severe bout of 'separation anxiety'. My daughter was leaving home and she was only eleven years old! I certainly wasn't going to be there to protect her, so who would? My mind was bombarded with questions. I wouldn't be able to tuck her in safely at night. How would I know when she was upset? I had to let my daughter leave my side and become who she was destined to be.

One day, I was driving Lisa to one of her regular outpatients' appointments in London. With tears pouring down my cheeks, I was amazed that I could see where I was going and we reached our destination without mishap.

Over the next few days I began to work through my emotions, and one by one, handed my anxieties, doubts and fears over to God. I began to feel more at peace about Lisa sleeping away from home.

As my anxiety abated so did my physical symptoms. Acquainted with the fact my daughter would soon relocate to a residential school, things were progressing nicely.

Or so it seemed.

CHAPTER TWENTY-SIX

Broken Bones

I placed a few family photos in a frame to keep beside Lisa's bed at school and asked her which toys and books she wanted to take with her. Outside of normal school hours, children wore their own clothes and it felt odd to pack a small suitcase for Lisa to take with her. Explaining to the boys that their sister was going to a residential school and would be home each weekend, Jamie, aged nine, said although he was going to miss Lisa, he knew it was the best thing for her.

The day before Lisa was due to leave home, all of a sudden, I felt totally overwhelmed and panic-stricken. Moments later the words *'Your child is deaf!'* blasted through me like a siren. I was afraid to let her go. What if something happened to her?

I picked up the telephone and asked my pastor if he could come and see me. I must have sounded desperate because that evening, when the children were in bed, he arrived on my doorstep, accompanied by a woman from church. After we prayed together, the pastor asked me, 'Have you forgiven God?' I was shocked. I thought it was the other way around, that I needed God to forgive me!

The more he shared, the more I came to see that I did need to forgive God. I blamed Him for giving me a disabled child with a terminal condition and hearing loss. As soon as I said the words, 'God, I forgive You,' a huge weight lifted off me and the stress fell away. Realising that I was not abandoning my daughter, the guilt went too.

The following morning Lisa said goodbye to her brothers, with lots of hugs, and then I drove my daughter to school. The staff and I agreed that it would be better if Lisa spent just one night there to begin with to gradually get used to the idea of sleeping away from home. The next day was Friday and I would go to collect her. Then we would have the whole weekend to chat about her two days in school. Lisa did not appear the least bit anxious or afraid.

On our arrival at school, I accompanied Lisa to her new bedroom, unpacked her suitcase, and placed the picture frame beside her bed. Our family photos included one of Lisa and her brothers having lots of fun splashing around in a paddling pool. I hoped that seeing our happy faces would help Lisa to feel less homesick and reassure her that we weren't too far away.

Making sure that my daughter was settling into her new environment and had everything she needed, I said my goodbyes and set off home. My apprehension was mingled with a sense of relief. Caring for Lisa left me physically and emotionally drained and having her stay in school four nights a week was definitely going to make life a whole lot easier.

Spending the first night at home without my beloved daughter was strange. I couldn't text or call her; the only way I had of knowing how Lisa was doing at school was to either speak to the staff or wait until Lisa came home.

It seemed that Lisa was happy in her new school. The staff kept close links with parents via a school-home book, and each Friday afternoon sent a general report on how Lisa was doing in the classroom and how she was coping amongst her peers, with relevant school news and extracurricular activities Lisa was involved in. In return, I kept the staff updated regarding any changes in Lisa's condition, plus family news from over the weekend.

We all looked forward to Fridays because Lisa would be home again, and I would cook her favourite meal of fried chicken and chips. It was so good to catch up with her news, although she wasn't able to tell us everything because of her lack of signing. Lisa appeared to be settling in well to her new environment.

Overall, I was pleased with Lisa's progress at school. She was adjusting to new technology in the classroom, designed for children with hearing loss. Each Friday when Lisa returned home she didn't seem to have any complaints, but with so much being new and unfamiliar to her she felt homesick and missed her family. I was delighted to hear that Lisa was beginning to make new friends, something I had longed for. At last my daughter was able to communicate with her peers. Lisa was eating well at school too, which was a relief to hear. Throughout her first year, there didn't seem to be any cause for concern.

One Friday afternoon when Lisa returned home from school, I was surprised to discover some bruising on her left knee and thigh. When I phoned the school, I was asked to call back the following Monday and speak to the member of staff on duty the previous week. It seemed best to visit the school in person, and the following Monday I spoke to a member of staff who shed some light on the subject. It turned out the major culprit was the electric wheelchair at school. The joystick used to control the wheelchair's movements was sensitive to the touch, making it jolt when moving forward or turning left or right. Occasionally when Lisa tried to go through a doorway she would crash heavily into the doorframe and bang her knee against the wood. Another probable cause of injury was the wheelchair itself. Between the armrest and the seat was a vertical metal rod which Lisa's thigh sometimes bashed against, hence the bruising.

The moment I saw Lisa in the wheelchair, it was obvious she wasn't sitting correctly. At her previous school, regular assessments were made and cushions provided to ensure Lisa maintain the correct posture – sat upright with both knees together, and the soles of her feet on the footplates. However, this was no longer the case. Her legs were splayed apart, her left knee jutting out to the side, making it prone to injury. The footplates were not at the correct height, either; they were too low and Lisa's feet couldn't reach them properly, only the balls of each foot touching the footplate instead of the soles.

Something was clearly amiss. Had an occupational therapist been to visit Lisa at school? Was the physiotherapist who visited the school aware of the problem? I was beginning to see gaps in the system. It was obvious Lisa's physical needs were not being met, but who was accountable? The teachers were clearly qualified to educate deaf and hearing-impaired children, but I began to have my doubts regarding how the school catered for children with additional physical handicaps. Whose responsibility was it to make sure my daughter's physical needs were being monitored and the necessary resources provided? Apparently, the school's physiotherapist had taken maternity leave and would not be returning. Lisa wasn't the only child in the school requiring regular physiotherapy, and a number of parents were not pleased that the physiotherapist had not been replaced.

During the next parents' meeting at school, the issue was raised as to why the former physiotherapist had not been replaced. Putting my case forward, it was clear from other parents' comments that I was not the only one dissatisfied with the situation. We were adamant that another physiotherapist should be provided. Drawing my comments to a close, people began to applaud and stood to their feet. I must have made quite an impression, because I was asked to become a parent governor and was duly elected. Thanks to the combined efforts of parents and staff, arrangements were made for a physiotherapist to visit the school on a regular basis.

A few months later, I noticed a distinct change in Lisa's behaviour. Returning to school on Monday had never been a problem for Lisa before, but on one particular occasion she seemed reluctant to go. It made me wonder what was going on, and I made a note of it in the school-home book. Her teacher assured me they would look into the matter and get back to me. The following Friday when I collected Lisa from the taxi, she seemed relieved to be home, more so than usual.

The following Monday morning, when I put Lisa into the taxi, I was shocked when a tear fell down her cheek. She hardly ever cried. Convinced that she wasn't in pain, I tried to ascertain why she was upset. But she couldn't tell me. Unable to keep Lisa at home that day, I assured her that I would telephone the school and ask them if they had any idea why my daughter was upset.

Watching the taxi drive away with Lisa sat on the back seat was not easy. A member of staff informed me that the school had recently accepted a number of pupils with learning difficulties, one of whom had 'challenging behaviour', and some had autism. Apparently, one of the boys had taken quite a shine to Lisa but in his enthusiasm, was far too heavy-handed with her, which she didn't like at all. Lisa was already thin from muscle wasting and lacked the strength to fend him off. The members of staff were far too busy to keep an eye on the boy all day, and I just couldn't see a way to resolve our predicament.

I wondered if I should remove Lisa from the school altogether; but where else could she go? It seemed unfair to me that Lisa should be the one that had to leave, because up to that point she seemed content and was thriving academically and socially and her self-worth had increased. This needed to be resolved, sooner rather than later.

When Lisa returned home the following Friday and I took off her coat, I immediately noticed the plastic splint around her wrist and wondered what it was for. Carefully pulling up her sleeve, I was in for a nasty surprise. Lisa's right forearm was literally bent upwards in the middle! It looked like it was broken. When I asked Lisa, 'Does your arm hurt?' she nodded. Without a moment's hesitation, I asked my next-door neighbour to look after the boys and drove Lisa straight to the hospital.

When I saw the results of Lisa's X-ray I was horrified. Lisa's right forearm was broken, the radius and ulna snapped in two. At first, I was stunned and then a surge of anger rose within me. No one at the school had informed me that Lisa's arm had been injured, let alone broken. And why was she only wearing a small splint on her wrist? Had anyone taken Lisa to see a GP? Had she been to the hospital already?

A 'both bones' fracture of the forearm often leads to surgery, and a metal plate and screws inserted into the bone. However, Lisa's case prompted further discussion between some doctors, an anaesthetist and the orthopaedic consultant to ascertain the risks involved in anaesthetising a child with Lisa's condition. They sought the opinion of the muscle clinic doctors in London. How would a general anaesthetic affect Lisa's breathing? Would she recover from such invasive surgery?

Lisa and I sat alone in the small cubicle with the curtain pulled around us. She looked so tired. We waited and waited.

Three hours later a doctor returned with the verdict: it had been decided that in view of the possible risks involved, Lisa would not be going to the operating theatre and a plaster cast would be applied to her forearm instead. Although Lisa's bones would gradually knit together, they would never realign properly without surgery. Even with Lisa's decreased sensitivity in her limbs, she must have experienced some degree of pain from having her arm broken.

On returning home I settled Lisa down and telephoned the school. It was early evening and the day staff had already gone home. The person on the other end of the phone was sympathetic but couldn't tell me exactly what had happened because she didn't have the facts. However, she did tell me that Lisa's arm was broken on *Tuesday* that week. Incredulous, I exclaimed, 'What! Are you telling me that my daughter has been at school with a broken arm for *three days* and no one did anything about it?' I was so cross! There was nothing the woman could say in response, except, 'I'm sorry, but you'll have to phone back on Monday and speak to the principal.'

It was going to be a very long weekend.

On Monday morning, I telephoned the school and spoke to the principal. Mr Jones listened patiently while I expressed my shock and horror in discovering that my daughter had been sent home with a broken arm. He explained the sequence of events. It was worse than I thought. One of the new intake of boys had grabbed hold of Lisa's arm with both hands and literally snapped her bones in two.

The school for the deaf already had guidelines in place regarding the necessary procedure when a pupil or member of staff sustained an injury, or was taken ill. On the day Lisa's injury occurred, the people who would normally have taken the appropriate action were all absent from school. Being short-staffed, there was no one available to take Lisa to see the GP or accompany her to hospital.

'Why didn't someone phone me?'

'I don't know, it's just one of those things,' he replied. 'I can understand why you're so upset. All I can do is offer you my deepest apologies. We will be putting the appropriate measures in place to make sure it doesn't happen again.'

It took me a while to simmer down, but what else could I do? I had too much on my plate already and the thought of taking legal action was more than I could bear. I'm sure the boy wasn't being malicious when he broke Lisa's arm.

The staff at Lisa's school worked incredibly hard; they often did overtime for extracurricular activities. It takes dedication to be a teacher and I'm confident the pupils flourished under their tuition and guidance. Lisa's care workers did the best they could with the resources available. At the same time, I began to have serious doubts regarding whether the staff had received adequate training to work with children who had learning difficulties.

CHAPTER TWENTY-SEVEN

Never Say 'Never'

An appointment was made for Lisa to have a muscle biopsy at the London hospital, and on that particular day we were accompanied by a friend. When I reached the car park, I looked for a sizeable gap to unload the wheelchair.

Never having seen a muscle biopsy performed, I had no idea what to expect. A health care assistant led us to a dingy room without windows – a perfect match for how I was feeling.

A woman wearing a white coat arrived and explained the procedure. A local anaesthetic was to be injected into Lisa's thigh to numb the area, followed by a small incision, and then a piece of muscle tissue removed.

After the injection was administered, I assumed the medic would wait for a few minutes for the anaesthetic to take effect, but she didn't and, using a scalpel, made a small incision approximately half an inch in length. Lisa winced, and with tears in her eyes motioned for them to stop.

'Sorry, Lisa, it won't be long now,' the doctor responded, extracting a small sliver of muscle tissue and then placing it into a sterile container to be examined under a microscope.

I suddenly felt quite faint. Having worked as an auxiliary nurse I was used to witnessing medical procedures, but this was far from OK. The fact that I had to sit there while someone cut into my daughter's leg before the local anaesthetic had taken effect was beyond belief. At first I was angry, then overwhelmed. I had been through so much with Lisa already and couldn't bear to see her in pain, let alone crying. What was the point of it all, anyway? My child wasn't going to benefit from any research. This procedure pushed me over my limit, but I still put on a brave face for Lisa's sake.

By the time I reached the car park, my emotions were at such a pitch I thought I would explode. Needing to put some distance between everyone and everything, I asked my friend if she could sit with Lisa for a few minutes and strode to the centre of a large open space nearby. Completely alone with no one else in sight, I began to let go. I took a long, deep breath and the emotional magma forced its way to the surface. The 'I'm fine' façade was obliterated. Without a hint of self-consciousness, I opened my mouth and let out a long, loud, agonised scream.

Over time I concocted various methods to release the stress without causing injury to myself or anyone else. Sometimes I would rant and rave while driving on my own. It was good that no one else could hear me, although I sometimes got funny looks from other motorists. Emotional outbursts became noisy prayers too. I'm glad God can handle it. Punching the cushions and pillows in the privacy of my own home was another effective stress-buster.

Sometimes the reality of Lisa's condition would hit me unexpectedly. One day I was sat at home watching an old movie on television. During the film, a young girl ran down the stairs, full of excitement, because she was going to a friend's birthday party and wanted to show off her new dress to her parents. The realisation that I had never seen Lisa run down the stairs in a party dress was like a hefty slap across the face.

I would never see my daughter walk down the aisle on her wedding day.

Lisa would never be able to have children.

That said, Lisa was prepared to have a go at the least expected challenges. One brisk spring day, Lisa was burning rubber on a cycle track in her electric wheelchair, chasing Jamie on his bicycle, with Luke following behind on his rollerblades trying to keep up. After an hour or so, we relocated to the play park to meet my sister there. My boys scampered up the climbing frame, agile as monkeys, and then zoomed down the slide. Lisa was sat in her buggy, watching children run to and fro and playing with friends.

In the centre of the play park was a suspended log bridge: two parallel bars at waist height, with a set of logs beneath them forming a bridge approximately four inches off the ground. Each log was suspended from the parallel bar by a metal chain which meant the logs swung back and forth and side to side. Traversing the log bridge proved a wobbly experience, as one by one, children made repeated attempts to get across from one end to the other without falling off. Tentatively placing their right foot on the first log, then the left foot on the next log, and so on, their legs swung in opposite directions – one leg forwards and the other backwards – and they fell off the bridge. Eventually each child accepted defeat and ran off to play on another set of equipment.

Lisa gazed intently at the scene. Jamie and Luke also had a go but kept falling off midway. No one was able to cross the bridge successfully.

'It's a shame that Lisa will never be able to do that,' commented my sister.

My twelve-year-old daughter looked up at me and, pointing towards the log bridge, signed 'me on there'. Instead of remaining a spectator, which was so often the case, she wanted to take part in the exercise and I had no intention of stopping her.

Locking my daughter's full-leg calipers at the knee so she could stand upright, I placed my hands under her armpits and walked her to the log bridge. The parallel bars were just the right height for Lisa's forearms. Placing her right foot upon the first log, she leaned slightly forward and then positioned her left foot upon the next log without any help from me. It was a precious moment and my eyes began to well up with tears. A small crowd of onlookers gathered around the log bridge to watch the impossible made possible by a special needs child who refused to accept defeat.

My daughter seemed oblivious to the spectators. Tentatively placing her feet upon one swaying log at a time, she had managed to reach the halfway mark without falling off once. I could feel the tension mounting. Everyone was rooting for her and the atmosphere was permeated with encouragement and support. No one spoke.

Just five more steps to go . . .

Every now and then she would look up towards the end of the bridge, and then look down again, to see where to place her foot next. The intensive legwork was really hard for Lisa. She couldn't grip the parallel bars with her hands, but had to slide her forearms along the bar as she went along. Each manoeuvre pushed her muscles to the limit but she refused to quit.

Just two more steps to go . . .

My mind was doing somersaults with anticipation, while silently willing her onwards. 'Come on, Lisa, you can do it!' I refrained from calling out because I didn't want to break her concentration.

This was her big moment!

Just one more log to go . . .

Lisa took the final step. The crowd clapped and cheered in awe. Her mission accomplished, Lisa was radiant and smiling from ear to ear. Any preconceived notions of 'she'll never be able to do that' lay shattered upon the ground beneath the swaying log bridge.

I learned that day – never say 'never'.

CHAPTER TWENTY-EIGHT

Malta Revisited

According to a doctor, Lisa would do far better if she lived in a warmer climate where she would not be prone to chest infections in winter. Three years had passed since my holiday in Malta and I planned to return on a fact-finding mission. A newspaper holiday advertisement caught my eye and seemed like a good deal – two weeks in Malta half-board, plus a third week free. My children were thrilled to be going on holiday. Unbeknown to me at the time, my close friend Annie and her husband, James, had also booked the holiday for two weeks.

The boys had lots of questions about flying, and to allay any fears, we engaged in some play-acting where dining chairs became two rows of plane seats. Giving a brief explanation of what would happen when we boarded the plane, the four of us sat bobbing up and down as we taxied towards the runway, accompanied by the sound of engines preparing for take-off. As the imaginary plane began to climb, we all leaned backwards. The scene had Lisa in fits of laughter.

Organising a holiday abroad with a wheelchair-user requires a lot of careful planning. I informed the airline well in advance regarding Lisa and was assured that our needs would be met.

We arrived at the airport in plenty of time but the airline check-in staff had not been informed about Lisa. There was no way I could carry my thirteen-year-old up the aircraft's boarding stairs, so it was arranged for Lisa and I to be transported on the hydraulic 'ambulift'. We had to wait until all the passengers had boarded before we could get on the plane. By a strange coincidence, my friend Annie and her husband had booked the same flight and took Jamie and Luke under their wing. Concerned that her brothers had gone without her and she would be left behind, I explained to Lisa that we needed to use a special lift to reach the door. We eventually boarded the plane and took our seats beside the boys, at the front of the mid-section. Lisa's wheelchair was stowed in the cabin.

My children loved the experience of flying, especially the roar of the engines on take-off. Halfway through the flight, Lisa needed to use the toilet. I would have to carry her down the narrow aisle past all the seats. When I stood up and turned around, I was in for a surprise. Seated behind us were rows and rows of men with olive complexions and dark hair, all wearing identical jackets. It was Malta's national football team.

Carrying Lisa down the aisle without bashing anyone's head was quite a mission. When I opened the door of the toilet cubicle my first impression was: 'This is impossible!' There was hardly enough room for one person in there, let alone two. We managed somehow, but with barely any room to spare. If Lisa had been an adult, I would never have coped.

When the children looked out of the window and saw the island of Malta, surrounded by a stunning blue Mediterranean Sea, they couldn't wait to explore. When the plane had landed, Lisa and I had to wait for the other passengers to disembark before we could make our exit.

Our hotel was set on the mainland. Cascading fuchsia-pink flowers adorned cream-coloured walls. There were steps at the main entrance and a concrete ramp to the side, but it was short and steep, so pushing Lisa up the gradient was hard work.

When we got to reception, I discovered that the hotel was fully booked and our accommodation was no longer available.

All they could offer was a self-catering apartment – a twin bedroom for Lisa and me, open-plan lounge/diner with a small kitchenette including sink, cooker and fridge, and a family bathroom. The boys would sleep on two sofa beds in the lounge. Double doors led onto a private courtyard with stone paving, colourful plants in earthenware pots and a tree, enclosed by a high wall. The accommodation and outside space was such a bonus. The boys couldn't wait to explore the hotel and ran off down the corridor, with me and Lisa in hot pursuit. They were delighted to see an outdoor pool, but weren't impressed when Jamie dipped his hand into the water.

'It's flippin' freezing!'

It was springtime, after all.

Our holiday package included a week's free car hire and we took full advantage of it. The children were eager to get to the beach, which was just ten minutes by car.

My first attempt to push a wheelchair on sand did not go very well. We were getting nowhere fast. Tilting the wheelchair back slightly, I managed to drag it through the sand backwards, but it took some effort.

Our hotel had a games room on the first floor. As the boys were getting out of the lift, the doors closed on Luke's head. Jamie was hysterical with laughter, but his younger brother was not amused. On a separate occasion, Luke was in the lift on his own when it became stuck between two floors. I was relieved he didn't have to wait long before normal service was resumed.

During one of our trips to the local park, I was busy with Lisa and had my back turned when Luke climbed a tree and slipped, his foot stuck between two branches. Dangling upside down, his head more than four feet off the ground, I had no way of getting him down. However, a kind passer-by came to our aid and rescued him.

One evening, my friend Annie and her husband offered to look after the children while I took a short break. Someone had mentioned that the sunset over Dingli Cliffs was spectacular and I couldn't resist the opportunity to see it. Just a couple of miles' drive away, getting there would not be a problem. I was not disappointed. The scene was magnificent! The return journey took much longer than expected. Unable to figure out the one-way system, it took me forty-five minutes to reach our hotel.

The kerbs in Malta were steeper than in the UK. When crossing the road, I had to lower the wheelchair very carefully down the kerb without letting the main wheels drop suddenly with a thump. On reaching the other side of the road, I didn't know whether to place the front wheels on the pavement and then heave Lisa onto the kerb, or turn the wheelchair round and pull it up backwards. Stood beside a kerb one day, trying to figure out the best way to do it without hurting my back, a man suddenly appeared and asked if I needed help. Before I could reply, he quickly lifted the wheelchair onto the pavement, smiled and walked away. I was utterly amazed and very grateful.

A leaflet about an evangelical church caught my eye at the hotel's reception and I telephoned the contact number provided. The following Sunday, a van arrived to transport my family to the service. When we arrived at the venue my heart sank – the meeting was held on the first floor and I would have to carry Lisa up two flights of stairs. Suddenly four men appeared out of nowhere, picked up the wheelchair, and whisked Lisa up the stairs as if she were light as a feather.

I wanted to relocate to Malta!

The climate in Malta seemed ideal for Lisa's health, with an average temperature of 31°C in summer and 10°C in winter. During our stay on the island the temperature ranged between

18-24°C. Apart from the occasional rainy day, intermittent showers would come out of nowhere and then suddenly stop minutes later. The storms were powerful, and thunder claps shook the hotel.

On a quest to discover the possibility of our relocating there, I paid a visit to an estate agent and was informed about a school for children with special needs. My family could live on Malta as temporary residents for three months at a time, but would have to leave the island for at least twenty-four hours before returning. One suggestion was to take the ferry to Sicily for an overnight stay. With regard to finances, the Maltese government would only allow foreigners to relocate to Malta if they had sufficient capital funds. Selling my three-bedroom house in the UK and purchasing an apartment in Malta was very tempting indeed.

On our return to the UK, everything seemed to point towards moving. Seeking wise counsel from church leaders, they queried the practicalities. This stopped me dead in my tracks. With too many things to consider, not to mention Lisa having to wear a plastic chest brace in the hot Mediterranean climate, I decided the best thing for my family was to remain in the UK.

CHAPTER TWENTY-NINE

Angels

Once, when we were out for the day, my van was parked a short distance from a lake. Jamie and Luke jumped out while I attended to Lisa's electric wheelchair. As we headed towards the lake, Lisa went ahead at top speed and disappeared around the corner while I hurried after her with the boys in tow. The lake was clearly visible at the far end of the pedestrian walkway. Lisa was a good twenty feet ahead and moving quite fast.

A short distance away was a car park barrier to prevent cars from entering the pedestrian walkway. As Lisa hurtled towards the lake, she was looking backwards over her shoulder to make sure I was following behind. She was laughing, probably because I had to run to catch up with her, but she wasn't paying attention to where she was going and didn't realise she was headed straight for the barrier. The heavy metal pole was level with her forehead and looming up fast. Yelling and signing, 'Lisa, stop!' had no effect. I knew I couldn't reach my daughter in time. Seconds before the impact, I cried, 'God, no!'

Lisa turned her head around just in time to see the barrier right in front of her; but it was too late to stop. The frightful sound of rattling metal confirmed the pole had been struck. The wheelchair ground to a halt on the other side of the pole, three feet ahead. Lisa was perfectly still, not moving a muscle. Rushing up to her as fast as I could, I had no idea what I would find.

Breathless from the sudden dash, I checked her face and neck for signs of injury. There wasn't a single scratch or red mark anywhere. Lisa looked at me, completely nonplussed. There was no indication that she had hit her head on the metal pole, so what made it rattle? I was perplexed. I looked at the height of the barrier in relation to Lisa's height sat in the wheelchair and there was absolutely no way she could have passed underneath the barrier, even if she had leaned right back. So how did she manage to get from one side of the pole to the other in a matter of seconds? It remains a mystery.

On another occasion, when I went to get Lisa out of bed, I noticed a slightly blue tinge around the edge of her lips. When I telephoned our GP's surgery, I was informed the doctor was just about to leave, but would see Lisa if we could get there within the next ten minutes.

We had to move fast and there wasn't time to arrange a childminder to look after the boys. The surgery was only a seven-minute walk away, but I knew we could only get there on time if I pushed Luke, then three, in the buggy. Not having two pairs of hands, I couldn't push Lisa in her wheelchair, which meant she'd have to use the electric one. Jamie would have no trouble keeping up with the pace.

By the time we arrived at the GP's surgery, with just seconds to spare, Lisa's lips had turned pink again. The doctor checked her heart, lungs and blood oxygen levels. Everything seemed OK and no further treatment was required.

The journey home meant having to cross a busy main road, two lanes on either side, and two sets of pedestrian crossings. Stopping at the kerb, I asked Jamie to press the button to change the traffic lights to red. My children knew to wait for the 'green man' symbol before crossing the road. To prevent Lisa from driving her electric wheelchair into the road before the lights had changed, I switched the setting to manual. The pavement was level, so I assumed the wheelchair would remain stationary. I applied the brakes on Luke's buggy, but forgot to put the brakes on the wheelchair.

The traffic lights changed to red and the 'green man' light came on. I was so busy attending to the children that I hadn't noticed the traffic lights had changed and both lanes of cars had stopped at the red light. Having missed the opportunity to cross the road, we would have to wait.

Then something inexplicable happened. The traffic lights changed back to green but the cars remained stationary. At that moment, Luke dropped his toy car onto the ground and I bent to pick it up. While doing so, Lisa's wheelchair moved forwards all by itself, went down the sloped kerb and eventually came to a halt in the middle of the road.

There was no way Lisa could have driven the wheelchair herself because it was still set in 'manual'.

No one had pushed it either.

The drivers were very patient with us. There were two rows of traffic, but no one hooted their horns. We crossed the road and reached the other side without further incident.

If the motorists had driven forward when the lights were green, there was no doubt in my mind that Lisa would have been hit by a passing car.

Maybe the drivers thought it best to wait until we had all crossed the road safely.

Or perhaps there was an angel looking out for us.

CHAPTER THIRTY

Heavenly Visitors

In celebration of Lisa's thirteenth birthday we held a party for her at home. Family friends joined in the fun. The following morning, however, Lisa took a turn for the worse. Every few minutes she took a deep breath in to fill her lungs with oxygen. Her temperature was elevated. I had a horrible feeling in the pit of my stomach.

Placing Lisa into God's hands, I asked Him for the grace to deal with whatever might be coming next. I prayed for wisdom for the doctors and anything else I could think of. When I telephoned our GP, she was busy on a home visit and informed me she would be there for quite a while. She instructed me to phone her back if Lisa became any worse. I contacted our pastor and asked if the church elders could pray. The pastor came to our house and prayed for Lisa's healing.

Throughout the morning Lisa's breathing became more laboured. I laid her on the sofa and propped her up with pillows to try to help her breathing. She looked anxious. Trying to ascertain my daughter's symptoms using basic sign language wasn't easy.

'Have you pain?'

'No.'

'Hard to breathe?'

'Yes.'

I telephoned our GP again. She was still attending to the same patient. I told her Lisa was getting worse. She hadn't finished with her patient but would be here as soon as she could.

It seemed an interminable wait. I felt helpless. I reassured Lisa that the doctor would be coming soon. A couple of hours had passed since my initial phone call. A mild sense of panic began to set in. Lisa was becoming drowsy and this was not a good sign.

'What's the matter with Lisa? Is she poorly?' asked Jamie.

'Yes, she is, but don't worry, the doctor's coming.'

'Please, Jesus, make Lisa better,' prayed Jamie, and I knew that he was believing in his heart that He would.

Ten minutes later the doctor arrived and examined Lisa. She wasted no time. 'She needs to go to hospital.' She dialled 999 for an ambulance.

The paramedics were on their way and I had five minutes to come up with a plan. Who would look after my sons? It was time for a 'break-glass-in-emergency' prayer. Immediately, a name came to mind of a young man from church who lived a few doors up the road. I sent Jamie to fetch Graham and they returned within minutes. He was able to stay the night while I made arrangements for someone else to look after my boys for the next few days. Darting upstairs I packed an overnight bag.

The paramedics wrapped Lisa in a blanket, placed her on a chair and wheeled her to the ambulance. Lisa was sat upright on the stretcher and an oxygen mask applied while the paramedic monitored her vital signs. I said goodbye to the boys and gave them a hug, then jumped inside the ambulance.

Flashing blue lights reflected off buildings as the ambulance made its way to hospital. It all felt like it was happening in slow motion. All I could do was smile at Lisa in the hope of reassuring her that everything would be all right. But I wasn't all right. I needed someone to be there for me too. The sirens blared and my insides trembled.

On our arrival at hospital, Lisa was allocated a single room on the children's ward, directly opposite the nurses' station. The consultant paediatrician was paged. A nurse entered the room and put an oxygen mask on Lisa which included a medicated vapour spray to help open her airways. A doctor tried to insert an intravenous (IV) catheter needle into the back of Lisa's hand, but his repeated attempts were unsuccessful and made Lisa wince. Thankfully, a nurse took over and inserted the needle straightaway without any fuss. A dextrose saline drip was administered intravenously.

A clip-like sensor was placed on Lisa's fingertip to measure the amount of oxygen in her blood, known as pulse oximetry. Oxygen is passed from the lungs into the blood and carried by the haemoglobin within red blood cells to the rest of the body via the bloodstream. Normal blood oxygen levels are 95-100 per cent. Our bodies need this to function properly.

An oxygen saturation level (SATs) machine displayed the data in bright red numbers and made an intermittent beeping sound. The numbers on the monitor began to decrease – 94-93-92-91, then went down to 90. Anything below 95 is a cause for concern. When it reached 89 the monitor sounded an alarm and I became tense. The number slowly went back up again and the alarm stopped. I relaxed. It dropped back down to 88, the alarm went off again and my body tensed. This pattern repeated itself continually – tense-relax-tense-relax. The monitor demanded attention; I felt drawn to it like a magnet and kept checking the numbers.

As if that weren't enough, Lisa was trembling from head to foot. The nurse said it was an allergic reaction to the medicated vapour spray to aid her breathing, and switched off the spray.

Although conscious, Lisa appeared listless and drowsy. Sat on an armchair beside her bed, I gently held my daughter's hand.

'Mummy's here.'

Nothing would make me leave my daughter's side.

Now all we could do was wait.

It was getting dark outside. I hadn't eaten for hours and I longed for a cup of tea. The door opened and in walked Pastor Andrew and his wife, Sally. Placing two flasks on the windowsill, Sally said, 'Thought you might like these. It's hot water, so you can make yourself a cup of tea when you need one.' Alongside the flasks were a packet of teabags, sugar and a carton of milk. They seemed to know what I needed, and I was grateful.

'Hi, Lisa, how're you feeling?' enquired Andrew. Barely moving and too tired to respond, Lisa moved her head slightly and simply looked at him. Turning to me, he whispered, 'How is she? Do they know what's wrong with her?'

'We're still waiting to see the consultant,' I replied, wearily.

Our visitors stayed for a while and then said their goodbyes. Lisa and I were alone once more. Except for the haunting echo of the beeping machine.

At long last, the consultant paediatrician arrived, followed by two nurses. He examined his patient, listened to her lungs, and pronounced his verdict, the one I had been dreading all along: 'Lisa has a chest infection; and she's got pneumonia too.'

I was too stunned to speak. Words of a London doctor from years ago came flooding back – if Lisa were to get a chest infection, it could be serious . . . even fatal.

Lisa motioned that she felt sick, and a few minutes later vomited some thick mucus tinged with green. Lacking sufficient muscle power to cough and clear her airways, she began to choke. I pressed the green call button on the wall to summon a nurse, but no one came. Lisa's SATs level was dropping steadily.

Opening the door, I called, 'Help!'

The nurses' station was across the corridor but no one was there. I pressed the green button again. Still no response. The monitor alarm beeped continuously.

Lisa began to panic. She was struggling to breathe and her face was turning blue. Pressing the green call button had had no effect and in desperation I pressed the red button instead. Within minutes the door flung open and a flurry of white coats and blue dresses swept into the room, one of them pushing a trolley laden with equipment. It was the crash team, responding to a cardiac arrest. Or so they thought.

Lisa's face was now dark blue. She was hypoxic, her body deprived of oxygen. Unable to breathe and thrashing about wildly, my child was fighting for her life. It took four adults to pin Lisa down on the bed and hold her still while the nurse attempted to insert a plastic airway into Lisa's mouth to suction the mucus out.

I was amazed at Lisa's strength. She continued to struggle and would not keep her head still, which made it difficult for the nurse to insert the airway to push a plastic tube through it and then down her throat. The doctor instructed the nurse to keep clearing the airway and the crash team vacated the room, one of them reprimanding me for pressing the red button as she left, which was for cardiac arrest only!

The nurse managed to get the plastic tube down Lisa's throat and suctioned the airway. Only a tiny amount of mucus came up; it was thick and sticky and therefore difficult to dislodge. After removing the airway briefly so Lisa could catch her breath, the nurse instructed me to hold Lisa's head still and reinserted the airway into her mouth, which made her gag.

'We don't usually do this to conscious patients,' said the nurse. 'Sorry, Lisa, this must be really unpleasant for you.'

My daughter had to endure the process of having an airway put into her mouth and a tube pushed down her throat four more times. Eventually her SATs level began to climb back up to the mid-90s. When the procedure was finally over, Lisa was sat propped up with pillows. She continued to inhale deeply to make up for the lack of oxygen.

When the nurse was satisfied with Lisa's blood oxygen levels, she left the room. My child was totally exhausted and fell into a deep sleep.

Standing at the foot of the bed, I suddenly felt faint and wrapped my fingers around the cold metal bar to stop me from keeling over. Traumatised, my body shook from head to foot. I gasped, 'Please God, send me someone from church. *Now!*'

No sooner had I completed the sentence, the door opened and in walked my friend Debbie. Although relieved to see her, I could not say a word. Debbie took one look at me and asked, 'What's wrong?' Lisa was still fast asleep. My friend put her arms around me and I burst into tears. When I couldn't cry any more, I explained what had happened. She made me a cup of tea, sat with us for a while and then left me to rest.

It was late evening now. Placing a roll-up mattress on the floor, I longed for sleep but the beeping SATs machine grated on my nerves. Try as I might, I just couldn't get to sleep, the nightmarish scenes playing over and over again in my mind.

For the next few hours I tossed and turned on the lumpy mattress, unable to get comfortable. I didn't really want to sleep in case Lisa woke up. The room was bathed in darkness, except for the faint glow of the night light above the hospital bed. I somehow managed to drift off to sleep for the next hour or two.

When I awoke, I quickly pulled myself onto my feet to make sure that Lisa was OK. She looked pale and thin, her eyes sunken and still fast asleep. Her SATs were in the low 90s. Dropping onto the floor, all I could do was pray. Drained to the core physically, mentally and emotionally, I simply couldn't take any more. I had come to the end of myself and I knew it. My resource reservoir was empty.

I glanced at the clock. It was past midnight and I was wide awake. It was pitch-black outside.

Just then, I thought I heard the sound of a trumpet blast followed by an angelic presence coming in the room. There was a distinct change in the atmosphere and I was tingling from head to foot.

Moments later, I saw Jesus coming into our room, His presence so glorious I could neither move nor speak.

My heart reached out to Him and my body was strengthened.

And then He spoke, the authority in His voice leaving no question as to who was in command.

Turning towards Lisa, Jesus boldly commanded, 'No evil shall dwell in this tent!'

In the New Testament, a 'tent' refers to a human body,[10] in which the spirit and soul reside.

Our room was saturated in the Lord's peace.

I lay there for what seemed like an hour; but it was only a few minutes. As suddenly as they had appeared, my heavenly visitors left.

Straightaway Lisa's SAT level began to rise and I *knew* that her lungs were healed.

It was the dawn of a brand-new day. When Lisa woke up she was radiant, with sparkling eyes and a big smile on her face. She was thirsty and asked for a drink, swallowing a whole glass of water with gusto, followed by another. She was hungry and asked for something to eat. The transformation was remarkable.

The intravenous needle in the back of Lisa's hand had become dislodged from the vein and her hand was swollen, the glucose solution having leaked into her tissues. I didn't want

10. See for example 2 Corinthians 5:1.

Lisa to endure having a needle inserted into the back of her hand again, so I asked God to intervene. A few minutes later the IV pump on the drip stand went 'bang!' followed by a puff of smoke. There was no need to set up another drip because Lisa didn't need it any more.

Later that morning the consultant arrived and examined Lisa. Judging by the look on his face, he was surprised at her rapid recovery.

'Well, Lisa, you seem a lot better! Your lungs are clear and I don't see why you shouldn't go home at this rate, but I want you to drink three more glasses of water before I let you go, OK?'

The consultant gave me a quizzical look. All I could do was smile and say, 'Jesus healed her.'

He scratched his head as he walked out the door.

'There's no denying that *something* happened here last night,' he said.

When I informed Lisa that she had to drink three more glasses of water before she could go home, she happily obliged and was discharged from hospital.

CHAPTER THIRTY-ONE

A Familiar Mountain

Lisa had recovered from pneumonia and was back at home when I received an unexpected phone call from the school principal. Mr Jones regretted to inform me that his staff could no longer cater for Lisa's physical needs and I would have to make arrangements for her to go elsewhere. When I told Lisa that she wouldn't be returning to the school, she seemed relieved. Faced with the prospect of trying to find another school, I had no idea where to start. We had faced this mountain before.

There was a school for children with special needs in my home town, except they catered for children with complex learning difficulties, sensory impairment and severe physical disabilities. It was the same school in which I completed my work experience, at the age of seventeen.

My daughter's learning difficulties, however, were only moderate. Placing Lisa in a school for severely disabled children was far from ideal. After doing so well at the school for the deaf, it seemed a huge backward step to put her in an environment where the children weren't able to communicate with her and her education might suffer because of a lack of resources. I was concerned she would be isolated again, but my hands were tied and there was nothing I could do.

The school was just a five-minute drive from our house but as the school car park would be so crammed with minibuses, children and walking aids, it was suggested Lisa be transported on the school bus. It seemed like a good idea at the time. With the school being just over a mile away, I naturally assumed that Lisa would be the last child to be picked up in the mornings and the first to be dropped off in the afternoons. Unfortunately for Lisa it was the other way around. She was the first child to be picked up in the mornings, which meant getting up really early and sitting on the bus while it drove here, there and everywhere collecting children from various towns along the way. After school, Lisa had to wait until everyone else had been taken home before she was dropped off. This didn't make sense to me, because she lived so close to school! When I asked the minibus driver if Lisa could be picked up last in the mornings and dropped off first in the afternoons, she was adamant that the route could not be changed. Apparently, the driver had no say in the matter, because the transport policy was devised by the powers-that-be in government officialdom. So that was that.

Lisa appeared to be settling into her new school environment quite well. Her teacher, Mrs Fields, was friendly and approachable and assured me that if I had any concerns about Lisa, I should not hesitate to go to see her.

The teaching methods were very different from Lisa's former school. Unable to provide Lisa with a signing interpreter, she would just have to manage without. Trying to communicate with her peers was quite a challenge.

In spite of everything, my thirteen-year-old daughter, the only girl in a class of fifteen, was very popular with the boys. One day, Mrs Fields approached me with a big smile and informed me that Lisa had received no less than three marriage proposals from her classmates!

My daughter loved being in the indoor heated swimming pool, aided by an assistant to prevent her from swallowing too much water. She enjoyed floating on a sponge mat, lying on her tummy, propped up by her elbows. Afraid of getting water into her lungs, she became agitated if anyone was splashing too close to her.

On one occasion, a couple of lads became overly excited and were hitting the water with lots of splashing. Lisa's classmates responded immediately. A group of them rushed over to her and surrounded the mat to prevent the lads from getting anywhere near. The majority of these children had severe learning disabilities and no one had instructed them to go to my daughter's aid.

Children with special needs never ceased to amaze me. The way they looked out for each other spoke volumes.

The occasional accident at school was not uncommon. One afternoon I received a telephone call to inform me that Lisa had cut her head and was in hospital. My heart pounding, I hurried to A&E and eventually found her behind a cubicle curtain, accompanied by a support assistant from school, who told me what happened.

Lisa had just completed her swimming and exercise programme when she was handed to a young assistant standing at the poolside. All of a sudden, Lisa slipped from her grasp and fell backwards, hitting her head on the hard-tiled floor. I was shocked that Lisa had been dropped, but accepted it was just an accident rather than negligence on their part. I explained to Lisa that she had a small cut on her head, about half an inch in length, and would need to sit still while the doctor stitched it back together. She was such a good girl during the procedure and I held her in my arms throughout.

The school staff worked incredibly hard. The children could be emotionally and physically demanding. Lifting a heavy child when they're a dead weight isn't easy, even with the help of lifting equipment, and back problems were commonplace.

On more than one occasion, I witnessed a child with severe learning difficulties lash out at a member of staff. In this profession bruises were par for the course, but the children would also give someone a hug when they least expected it, or plant a kiss on their cheek.

You were never quite sure what was coming next!

CHAPTER THIRTY-TWO

Together

When I was at school, the annual sports day made me cringe. When the netball captains took it in turns to pick their teammates from the line-up, I was usually one of the last to be selected. When I became a parent, however, I really enjoyed attending my children's sports days.

My sons' lower school held their sports day in the local park, the grass painted with white lines for the running lanes. The sun shone as mums and dads gathered alongside the tracks. Children aged between four and nine, clad in white T-shirts and shorts, drifted like clouds across the green, then sat cross-legged in their class groups on the far side, opposite the spectators. Eager faces scanned the audience hoping to catch sight of their family, waving frantically for their attention and calling out, 'Mum!' or 'Hi, Gran!' Grandparents enjoyed the event too, their presence appreciated by children whose parents were at work.

Grateful for the shade of a mature oak tree, I scanned the crowd of small fidgety people in search of six-year-old Luke. Intense concentration furrowed his brow as he searched for his mum and wondered, 'Is she here?' Suddenly our eyes locked and he broke into a smile, waving emphatically.

One by one, groups of children stood to their feet in preparation for the upcoming race. Five marched to the starting line and stood side by side in their allotted lane. Each team was identified by the colour of their badge. The children stood poised for action, waiting for the headteacher to give the command.

'Ready, steady, go!'

They were off.

Some glided effortlessly along the track as if carried on angels' wings, and others had to put in more effort. Shouts boomed from both sides of the tracks as children yelled for their teammates, and parents and friends cheered for their loved ones. Teachers encouraged children who lagged behind.

In the next race, a young boy took up position at the starting line. He was running to win and second place was not an option. He sped effortlessly past the others, his family shouting from the sideline, 'Keep going!' At the halfway mark, he stumbled and crashed to the ground as his competitors sped past him. The race long over, all eyes were on the solitary figure lying on the track, curled into a foetal position with his knees against his chest, sorely disappointed.

When sports day was held at Lisa's school for children with special needs, I had no idea what to expect. The racetrack was marked out on the school playground, surrounded on three sides by the main building, and a few trees near the finishing line. The racetrack consisted of five short lanes from one end of the playground to the other. Various objects were placed on the ground at regular intervals. At the starting line was a small plastic bucket, and further along the track were beanbags, then balls and finally a large hoop. The spectators, which included family and friends, stood at the far end of the playground near the finishing line, eager for the first race to begin. Some of the children were a lot more coordinated then others, judging by the time it took them to pick up the various objects and place them in the bucket before stepping through the hoop and crossing the finishing line.

The schoolchildren were assembled along the far side of the race track watching their friends progress and cheering them on. Searching for Lisa amongst the children, the moment I saw her, my heart smiled. She was wearing her favourite T-shirt; on the front, there was a picture of a strong-looking angel with wings extended. Written beneath: 'He will command his angels concerning you to guard you in all your ways.'[11]

Lisa had an entourage of male admirers around her but her focus was on the competitors. When Lisa spotted me amongst the crowd, she acknowledged her pleasure by thrusting her torso forwards and backwards a couple of times against the wheelchair as if dancing. Lisa's smile caused the teacher beside her to glance in my direction, and when she saw me, she waved a friendly greeting. One of the boys in Lisa's suitor group bent towards her and got too close for comfort, receiving a hefty whack across his chest with Lisa's arm. He instantly complied and returned to his rightful place.

It was time for Lisa's race and her teacher pushed the wheelchair to the starting line.

They were off!

The teacher ran to and fro with the wheelchair, handing Lisa various objects to drop one by one into the red bucket at the starting line. Lisa found the teacher's antics highly amusing, and was laughing at being propelled across the playground at great speed. Their efforts were rewarded and she crossed the line in first place.

Watching the races was an uplifting experience, each disabled child trying their utmost, regardless of their ability, or lack of. The expression on their faces when they crossed the

---

11. Psalm 91:11, ESV.

finishing line was a joy to behold. They seemed happy with the outcome regardless of whether they came first, second or last. The level of concentration and the amount of effort put in was astounding.

Instead of hurdles there were wooden benches, approximately 30cm high. Some managed to clear them with minimal effort but, at the far end of the course, there was a young girl with Down's syndrome who took longer to jump over the benches and eventually came in last. Her jubilation on crossing the finishing line matched that of the winner's. Beaming with sheer delight, plus an exuberant 'yes, *yes!*' she ran to her mother and gave her a big hug, her proud mum responding, 'Well done!'

The next race was about to begin. Of the five who took their place at the starting line, they could all run, although some had better coordination than others. The set tasks – placing objects in a bucket, putting on various garments, jumping over hurdles, and finally stepping through hoops – would no doubt take a while. One boy in particular, aged thirteen or so, was falling behind the others, each task taking him longer to complete than his peers. The remaining four boys and girls were soon heading towards the finishing line. The young man at the front had successfully completed the tasks and was three feet from the finishing tape. He knew he would win the race and looked ecstatic.

A few strides from victory, the boy glanced over his shoulder as if looking for someone. His friend was way behind and struggling to put on a hat, scarf and gloves. The 'soon-to-be-winner' stopped in his tracks, turned around and ran back to his friend who was trailing in last place. The faithful friend came alongside the boy and encouraged him not to give up.

The remaining children were approaching the finishing line when they saw the would-be winner in front of them stop and run back past them, and they too went to help the boy.

Surrounding their classmate, they did what any good friend would do.

'Go on, you can do it!' they called out.

These remarkable children had no intention of leaving their friend behind, even if it meant sacrificing their own glory in winning the race. Their selfless attitude was finally rewarded as, little by little, the boy successfully completed his tasks and all five children made their way towards the goal.

It was an awe-inspiring scene and it brought tears to my eyes.

When they reached the tape, the children stood side by side, linked arms and crossed the finishing line.

Together.

CHAPTER THIRTY-THREE

Growing Up Fast

Given the choice, I don't suppose many teenage girls would go clothes shopping with their mothers. It would have been nice if Lisa could have gone into town with her friends to buy clothes, but she couldn't. What happens when a young disabled person looks in the mirror and thinks, 'Please don't make me wear that, I look awful,' but they can't express it? Youngsters will either gravitate towards a fashion trend, or come up with a style of their own. But they do have a choice. Young people with disabilities are no different. Lisa usually decided what she wanted to wear, unless we were running late and I quickly grabbed something out of the wardrobe.

Lisa's choice of clothing was determined by factors beyond the norm. For instance, there wasn't much point in her wearing a skirt and thick tights in winter because she'd get too cold. Spending most of her time sat in a wheelchair, she didn't generate enough body heat to keep warm, and being so thin didn't help, either. I don't know how Lisa felt about wearing her special shoes, AFOs and calipers because she couldn't tell me. I suppose it was her 'normal' and she didn't know any different.

When Lisa was fourteen, I took her to the opticians to purchase a new pair of glasses. The frames Lisa had chosen in the past were rather plain, but the new ones were just the opposite and resembled an explosion in a paint factory! They suited her personality, especially her quirky sense of humour.

The year before, when Lisa was thirteen, her quest for independence took a sudden turn and it knocked the wind right out of my sails. My friend Patricia was going out for the day and asked if I could go to her house and feed the dog. Her back garden was near the end of my street, just around the corner.

Benji the dog, left out in the garden, greeted us by running around in circles. I'm not sure whether he was excited to see us or knew it was feeding time. Probably the latter. My daughter liked dogs and thankfully Benji was easy to manage. I made sure to shut the garden gate so he didn't run away, and kept him outside while I prepared his dinner in the utility room. Every few seconds his head would appear through the pane of glass and then disappear again as if he was jumping on a trampoline, which made us laugh.

Benji devoured his food like an industrial vacuum cleaner.

'Where's your water bowl?' I asked, as if he could answer, and began to search the garden. I looked everywhere. After licking his dinner bowl scrupulously clean, Benji looked up at me as if to say, 'Is that it?' Resuming my search for the elusive bowl, I eventually discovered it under a bush.

Mission 'feed the dog' complete, it was time to return home, but Lisa was nowhere to be seen. I had been so preoccupied with the dog that I didn't realise my daughter had gone. The garden gate was wide open and my mind went into overdrive. What if someone had snuck into the garden and snatched my daughter when I wasn't looking? Was she in one of these houses? I began to panic. Every second counted.

'Lisa!' I called at the top of my voice, although she couldn't hear me anyway.

I closed the gate behind me and hurried off in search of my daughter. Maybe if I was quick enough I would see someone bundle Lisa into the back of a van and could quickly make a note of the registration number and then phone the police.

Adjacent to the garden was a portion of land with garages on either side used by local homeowners. I went over to check if Lisa was there. The garage doors were all closed except for one at the far end. My heart pounding, I ran over and looked inside. It was empty.

I looked up and down the street. There was no sign of Lisa anywhere. Beseeching God to help me, I hurried home and checked every front garden along the way.

My front door was open. I half-expected to find Lisa waiting for me inside, but there was no sign of her in the hallway, or the kitchen. My heart in my mouth, I darted into the lounge. There she was, sat in her electric wheelchair, as cool as a cucumber. I was shocked! And very relieved.

'Where were you?' I signed, in a fluster. 'I was looking *everywhere* for you!'

'What's wrong, Mum?' asked Jamie.

'I couldn't find her,' I said, exasperated. 'I didn't know where she'd gone!'

'It's OK, Mum, Lisa came home by herself.'

Jamie's words rang in my ears.

Lisa came home by herself.

She had never done anything like that before.

After putting my children to bed that evening, I sat and mulled over what had happened that day. Like her peers, Lisa had reached a stage in her life when she wanted to become more independent. To spread her wings and fly solo. She didn't want her mother to accompany her every time she went out. What teenager would? What was I supposed to do now? I went everywhere with Lisa. The only time we spent apart was in school time.

Becoming independent is a natural part of growing up. We endeavour to teach our children the dos and don'ts when they're out with friends because we want them to be safe, and hopefully they'll let us know if they're going to be home late. If they need help, or a lift somewhere, all they need do is ask. Girls phone their friends when they want to meet up and can hop on a bus to meet up at the shopping centre. Most girls can phone and say, 'Hi, Mum, I'll be back around six.' But not my Lisa. She couldn't get on a bus without assistance, or use the telephone.

Would I ever allow my disabled daughter to go into town and back on her own? What if there were steps outside the shop and she couldn't get her electric wheelchair inside; would anyone help her?

How could she purchase items when her fingers couldn't open her purse to get some money out?

What if her wheelchair toppled over?

How could she tell people if there was something wrong with her?

If she was hit by a car, how could she tell the paramedics and hospital staff where she lived?

How would I know if she was injured?

What if she were assaulted or abducted?

What if she was raped or murdered?

As far as I was concerned, it all boiled down to one thing – my daughter was unable to defend herself. She couldn't call for help, or scream, or fight a person off, or run away. Lisa would be completely vulnerable to whoever or whatever came her way.

I was faced with an impossible situation. Was I being irrational? If I were to let my daughter go out on her own without my being there to watch her every move, even from a distance, I knew I would be fraught with worry until she returned home in one piece. For me, the worst part would be not knowing if she was OK or not, and I wouldn't know one way or the other until she was back at home, safe and sound.

I couldn't do it. I couldn't take the chance. If I did let my beautiful daughter go out alone and something awful happened to her, how would I ever forgive myself? The prospect of my teenage daughter becoming independent was overwhelming. I just couldn't face the possible scenarios, and all the 'what ifs'.

In the quiet of the evening I poured my fearful heart out to God, sobbing, 'I can't do it, it's too much!' Deep down on the inside I knew, beyond all doubt, that to let my daughter go out on her own was more than I could bear.

CHAPTER THIRTY-FOUR

Letting Go

Without a partner to share the load, there were times when the weight of responsibility in caring for a family and running a household was crushing. Lisa took up most of my energy, but my role as a single mother included that of cook, cleaner, nurse, laundry-maid, painter and decorator, gardener and taxi driver. Not to mention trying to keep on top of the household bills.

Under pressure and in desperate need of help, I contacted Social Services, who arranged for a home help to give me a hand for a couple of hours, once a week. Mary was an absolute treasure and the children were fond of her too. A retired woman, our home help from heaven zoomed around the house with the vacuum, dusted and did some cleaning here and there. She was also more than happy to do a bit of food shopping when I needed to remain at home with Lisa. Having someone help with the housework made a huge difference and I don't know how I ever managed without her. Having said that, I couldn't expect her to look after Lisa for me, and I was desperate for a break.

As Lisa's muscle wasting progressed I became increasingly tired, both physically and emotionally. I longed for someone to sit with Lisa so I could go out for an hour or two. Apart from friends paying a visit every now and then, my social life outside the house was virtually nonexistent.

Our local council launched a 'shared care scheme' that provided fully trained and approved carers to look after a disabled child whilst their families took a break for an hour or so, or went away for the weekend. There was also an option for the child to spend a few days away from home accompanied by the carer, to enable the rest of the family to enjoy some respite in their own home.

After making a few enquiries and filling out the necessary forms, I was delighted to be informed that my family was eligible and a carer would be provided for Lisa. Various questions popped into my mind. Would we get on? Could I ever trust a stranger to take care of my daughter? Would Lisa be OK with her?

Arrangements were made for the carer to pay us a home visit so that we could get to know one another. I couldn't wait to meet her but I was a little apprehensive too. When our carer arrived, I could not believe my eyes. Standing on the doorstep, a big smile on her face, was my friend Amanda! Unbeknown to me she had already been accepted onto the scheme.

When she discovered that she would be looking after Lisa, Amanda had wanted it to be a surprise. It was the perfect solution. Not only had we been friends for years, our children played together often, and Amanda was a qualified nurse!

At long last, I could take a much-needed break, resting in the fact that Lisa was in the best possible hands. All I had to do was let go and trust others.

It's hard to let go of your children. I knew that my daughter had a life-limiting condition, but in my heart I was hanging on to her for dear life. There comes a time when you have to face facts, however painful.

Lisa was twelve when I first experienced a gentle whisper in my soul telling me to *let go*. I knew what it meant straightaway. I was being prepared for the day when Lisa would return to heaven. I responded with a resolute: 'NO!'

I wasn't ready.

Would I ever be?

How could I possibly come to the place where I could, or would, accept that my daughter was going to die?

Family life seemed to revolve around Lisa. Each day I would plan ahead to ensure I was ready to meet her every need. The next hospital visit was always in the back of my mind. Whatever I did with the children, wherever we went, I first had to think 'wheelchair' just to make sure the trip was even possible.

I didn't tell anyone about the inner prompting to 'let go'. I refused to say the words, thinking that it might set things in motion or, God forbid, it meant that Lisa was going to die soon. Even the thought of it was too much. So, I held on tight. Nothing was going to change my mind.

I placed this thought deep in my soul's basement, where it remained hidden. No one was allowed access. I refused to consider the notion that I had to let go of my daughter. I wasn't ready.

Another year passed before I experienced the same quiet voice on the inside, saying 'let go'.

Little by little, I began to yield.

In 1995, I heard the words 'let go' for the third and final time, spoken in the same gentle and loving manner.

But this time my response was different.

I did not put up a fight.

Somehow, I knew that my beloved daughter would soon be on her way to heaven.

CHAPTER THIRTY-FIVE

The Beginning of the End

In the summer of 1995 I was on holiday with my children when Lisa's condition took a turn for the worse. She was fourteen. A charity had kindly paid for my family to spend a week at a holiday camp on the south coast of England. Before making the booking, I had telephoned to make sure that the venue was suitable for wheelchairs, and their representative assured me that it was. On our arrival, the reality was very different. I was shocked to discover a steep gradient that would restrict our movements around the camp. However, I was accompanied by a young lady from church, a much-needed spare pair of hands, and she was happy to take the boys swimming while I tended to Lisa.

One afternoon towards the end of the holiday, Lisa and I were sitting in the caravan when I noticed a distinct change in her breathing. Her respiration rate had increased and she was taking deep breaths, as if she was running up a hill. Lisa had been sitting still, so I wondered why her body required that much oxygen. There was no sign of a blue tinge on her lips. My daughter looked up at me with her big brown eyes, as if to say, 'What's wrong with me?' I knew I had to remain calm and reassuring, but this new development in her condition worried me. I had never seen anything like it before.

That morning, people from church had gathered for the weekly prayer group. Rushing to a telephone box on the campsite,

I phoned a friend and told her about the sudden change in Lisa's condition and asked the group to pray.

'Do you think it's serious?' asked my friend.

I paused for a few moments and then replied, 'Yes.'

I thought it best not to say anything to the children and by the grace of God I managed to keep it all together for the remainder of the holiday. Deep in my heart I knew what was happening. It was the beginning of the end.

One evening a few months later, I noticed that Lisa was a little blue around her lips and I took her to our local hospital to have her blood oxygen levels checked. As I waited to see the doctor, the Lord spoke to my heart very clearly: 'I am the resurrection and the life.'[12] His words stopped me dead in my tracks. It confirmed what I already knew. Lisa would be going to heaven soon. I wasn't agitated or fearful because I knew where she was going. Death was not the end.

Lisa's oxygen levels stabilised and she was given the all-clear to go home. We spent the next few hours waiting for hospital transport and didn't get back until the early hours of the morning. As I put Lisa to bed, she put a hand to her ear a few times and asked, 'What's that noise?' Although she was hearing impaired, it seemed that she had heard something.

Using sign language, I asked, 'What can you hear?'

She replied, 'Jesus is talking to me.' A little later, she said, 'Tell me about heaven.'

Deep down I sensed that God was preparing her. Instead of being troubled, I felt a deep sense of calm. In simple terms, I explained as best I could.

'In heaven there is no pain, and people are happy. It's filled with beautiful colours; and Jesus lives there.'

I knew it was time to ask the question.

---

12. John 11:25, NKJV.

'Do you want to go to heaven and be with Jesus, or do you want to stay here with Mummy?'

I braced myself for her response.

Lisa simply replied, 'Stay here with Mummy.'

Lisa attended the school for severely disabled children for more than a year and seemed relatively happy there. As the summer term began to draw to a close, I was asked to visit the school and speak with Lisa's teacher, who explained that my daughter would be moving to a different class in September. This was disappointing news because Mrs Fields had a special rapport with the children and they responded well to her. She asked if I would like to see Lisa's new classroom and meet the teacher and I accepted her offer. I was in for quite a shock.

The teacher seemed quite pleasant. The classroom consisted of six young teenagers, all of whom were severely disabled. My first impressions were not good. These youngsters could barely communicate at all! I envisaged Lisa sitting there, cut off and unable to integrate. I knew beyond all doubt that it was not the right environment for her, but the school was already short-staffed due to funding cutbacks and there was nothing they could do about it. Lisa would have to go into the class, like it or not.

What was I supposed to do now? As far as I was aware, there wasn't another school in the county that could meet Lisa's needs, so I was back to square one again. The school for the deaf had reluctantly turned Lisa away because they couldn't cope with her physical condition any more. The staff at Lisa's current school were more than qualified to work with severely disabled children, but Lisa did not have severe learning difficulties and they couldn't provide a qualified signing interpreter. Lisa was a square peg in a round hole, but where else could she go? Once again, the search was on.

The headteacher informed me about a special school in the same county and suggested that I make enquiries.

Arrangements were made for me and Lisa to pay them a visit. The school wasn't too far away, just thirty minutes by car. First impressions were very positive. The children, aged between three and nineteen, had a range of physical disabilities, plus learning and communication difficulties. The teachers, who were very friendly and welcoming, were more than happy for me and Lisa to have a look around the classrooms. The first thing that struck me was the bright and cheery atmosphere. The classrooms were well-equipped and the teachers covered a wide range of specialist subjects. The hydrotherapy pool was definitely a bonus for Lisa. I wondered why I hadn't been told about this school before.

Lisa was offered a placement in September and I was delighted. She was enthusiastic about going there too. A member of staff suggested that because Lisa needed a signing interpreter, I should put in a request with the LEA for an educational communicator to be assigned full-time. That was news to me because I had always been led to believe that Lisa was only entitled to an interpreter on a part-time basis. Asking the LEA to transfer my child to another school was one thing, but requesting a full-time educational communicator too?

I needed a miracle and I knew just the person to ask.

The staff at Lisa's current school backed my decision and their support was invaluable. With half the battle won already, Lisa's case was presented to the powers-that-be. My application was successful. Lisa could go to the school and the LEA would pay for a full-time educational communicator to translate for her!

When Lisa started at her new school she was two months away from her fifteenth birthday. The journey to get this far had been long and at times arduous, but Lisa would now receive the support she needed as a physically disabled child with moderate learning difficulties and a hearing loss, in a school which had the facilities and expertise to enable her to make the most of the time she had left.

The school bus picked Lisa up every morning, Monday to Friday, and brought her home in the afternoon. Children were collected along the way, so the journey took more than thirty minutes. Lisa wasn't too keen on being woken up at seven o'clock in the morning and couldn't face eating any breakfast before she went to school.

On Lisa's fifteenth birthday one of my friends made her a lovely birthday cake. Similar to a mixed-fruit Christmas cake covered with marzipan and white icing, it was decorated with pale pink and white flowers and was by far the tastiest cake I had ever eaten. Lisa thoroughly enjoyed it, so much so that she wanted to eat a slice of cake every morning for breakfast!

Most days when Lisa came home from school, she looked tired. The first thing I did was to give her a drink, remove her chest brace and lay her on the sofa with her head propped up with a cushion so she could rest a while. Lisa had a wonderful sense of humour even when she was tired. Her antics made us all laugh, especially the funny faces she pulled as she lay on the sofa. In spite of the fact that her body was slowly being ravaged by a horrible wasting disease, her spirit was becoming stronger every day. Lisa glowed from the inside out.

After a while, I paid a visit to the school to see how Lisa was settling in and I was delighted to meet her new signing interpreter. Sarah was a lovely lady in her early thirties who was profoundly deaf. I was intrigued. How could a person who was born without hearing become a fully qualified signing interpreter for the deaf? Sarah was a huge inspiration to me. She probably understood my daughter far better than anyone else. The rapport between Sarah and Lisa was very special. I wished Lisa had been provided with a full-time communicator years before. She had missed out on so much over the years.

My daughter blossomed in her new school. She was happy in class, which I'm sure had a lot to do with the fact that she could understand what was being taught and could integrate with her peers like never before. The staff seemed fond of Lisa too, especially the class assistant, who took care of her personal needs each day.

Sessions in the hydrotherapy pool were one of Lisa's favourite activities. One day, when Lisa had been in the pool, I received a phone call asking me to come and fetch her. I was told she seemed breathless and the staff were concerned. When I arrived at the school, I discovered Lisa sat in the corridor laughing and joking with her assistant. Lisa seemed to have made a swift recovery and was now breathing normally again.

I was not at all prepared for what happened next.

CHAPTER THIRTY-SIX

The Day Lisa Died

Lisa's sudden attacks of rapid breathing were becoming more and more frequent, each bout lasting around ten minutes. Concerned about the recent development in her condition, I telephoned the London hospital and spoke to one of the muscle team doctors. Arrangements were made for Lisa to attend the outpatients' department the following morning to undergo a series of tests, and I was advised to bring an overnight bag, 'just in case'. We usually had to wait for weeks, if not months, for an appointment, and I was surprised that Lisa was asked to come in so soon. Things were moving fast.

On previous occasions, I had always driven to the hospital, but this time I asked my father to take us. As we sat in the corridor waiting to see the doctor, my father explained that he needed to leave because he had a meeting. He gave me a hug and then placed his arms around his granddaughter, and said, 'Goodbye, Lisa, your granddad loves you.' Lisa nodded and smiled. I discovered later that as my father walked away, he knew in his heart that he would never see his granddaughter again.

After about thirty minutes, a doctor appeared and led us into a side room, where I was surprised to see a team of doctors sitting behind a desk. Apparently, Lisa's condition was of interest to them and they wanted to witness a rapid breathing spell to find out what was going on, but Lisa seemed OK. Twenty minutes later, the doctors began to file out of the room and told me to call them if anything happened. One of the doctors stayed behind, asked me lots of questions and took notes. He then left the room too and Lisa and I were on our own.

Ten minutes later, my daughter's face turned red and she began to perspire, followed by rapid breathing. As instructed, I went to fetch a nurse and asked her to inform the doctors. A doctor arrived and hooked Lisa up to an electrocardiogram (ECG) machine to monitor the electrical activity in her heart. Three blood samples were also taken. It was agreed that Lisa should stay in overnight for observation and to run more tests. Lisa didn't seem to mind being admitted onto the children's ward, as long as I stayed with her. Jamie and Luke were staying the night at my father's house. As far as my boys were concerned, there was nothing unusual about Lisa going into hospital. It was quite a regular occurrence.

In spite of the fact that I had no idea what was coming next, I was strangely calm. Lisa was settling in well and didn't seem to be worried either.

That afternoon, when the food trolley arrived, Lisa asked for an egg sandwich, but when she took a bite, she had difficulty swallowing it. I looked into her mouth and noticed a piece of egg lodged at the back of her throat. As she was unable to cough, a nurse had to remove the food by suctioning it out with a tube. Lisa seemed to have lost the swallowing reflex. I wasn't prepared for that.

From the moment Lisa was admitted onto the ward, her condition began to deteriorate rapidly. Her skin turned pale yellow-grey in colour. A nurse informed me that Lisa's kidneys were failing.

I could see that Lisa was going downhill fast.

I sat beside her bed in the middle of the hustle and bustle of the children's ward. I felt exposed and wanted us to go somewhere quiet instead. A nurse came over and whispered, 'Would you like us to move Lisa into her own room?'

I knew what this meant.

All the side rooms were occupied and the only available bed was in the treatment room outside the children's ward. The room was also being used as a store room, with stacks of boxes along the walls. On the far side of the room, near the window, was a hospital bed.

Being mid-December, there were Christmas decorations hanging on the walls. At the foot of the bed was a huge star, approximately 50cm in diameter, made of gold and silver foil. An assortment of paper lanterns, candles and snowmen provided a welcome splash of colour to the room, and from the ceiling hung Christmas trees, puddings, Santas, reindeers, presents and sweets. I was grateful that Lisa had something nice to look at.

Our old friend the SATs machine provided the only sound in the room. The intermittent beeps felt like being poked every few seconds with a derisive, 'Your child is sick, your child is sick.' I glanced frequently at the screen to see what Lisa's blood oxygen levels were doing; I was continually on edge.

A glucose saline solution was administered intravenously to prevent dehydration.

The episodes of rapid breathing became more frequent, her chest heaving, draining her of energy.

As I sat on the chair beside my daughter's bed, I gently stroked her forehead and whispered, 'I love you.' The presence of God in the room was tangible. His peace saturated the atmosphere and provided the comfort we so desperately needed.

Later that afternoon, a hospital cleaner came into the room and began to sweep the floor around Lisa's bed. She asked me what was wrong with my daughter, but I didn't feel like talking and only said a few words. All of a sudden, the woman went into overdrive, boldly rebuking the devil and commanding him to leave my child alone. I'm sure she meant well, but I felt really uncomfortable at the unwelcome intrusion and wished that she would go away and leave us in peace. If I had thought for one minute that Jesus was going to perform a miracle and heal my daughter, then I would have prayed too, but I knew in my heart that Lisa was dying.

I refused to leave my daughter's side in case something happened while I was away. I wouldn't even go to the loo. At eleven o'clock in the evening the door opened and in walked the pastor from our church. A few months before, Pastor Jerry, his wife, Sandy, and their children had relocated to the UK from America to join the leadership team. Jerry was exactly what I needed and he offered to stay with Lisa while I took a short break. First I dashed to the toilet and then the hospital shop, purchasing a cup of coffee and a snack to keep me going through the night. I also bought a magazine; I wanted to give my head a rest from what was happening around me.

Jerry prayed quietly for Lisa and she settled down, then fell asleep. It was a much-needed respite for us both.

We were in for a long night.

At three o'clock in the morning Jerry suggested I have a rest while he kept watch over Lisa. I unfurled the mattress on the floor but I couldn't get to sleep, even though I was exhausted. I finally managed to doze off at four o'clock in the morning and awoke an hour and a half later.

Jerry was still in the armchair, wide awake. He had been up all night watching over Lisa and praying for our family. Jerry said he needed to return home, grab some breakfast and prepare for a meeting scheduled that morning. I expressed my heartfelt gratitude.

'If you need me,' he said, 'just call, and either myself or my wife will come.'

When Lisa woke up, her rapid breathing awoke with her. Sat on the chair beside her bed, I gently held her hand in mine. She looked so frail and helpless. That being said, she only weighed about 51lbs, well below the standard norm for someone her age and height (approximately four feet tall). And she would have been much thinner, were it not for the extra weight she had put on from eating so much birthday cake, just a few weeks before. She had been unable to eat anything since the previous morning and she must have felt very weak. The constant struggle of trying to breathe had worn her out.

Around mid-morning a nurse poked her head around the door and said, 'The doctor would like to speak with you in his office.' She offered to sit with Lisa while I went out.

The doctor informed me of a new drug which he believed would help to prevent Lisa's hyperventilation and restore her breathing back into a normal rhythm. A form of tranquilliser and still on trial, the doctors wanted to test the drug on my daughter. She would be given the correct dosage according to her bodyweight, and just to be on the safe side, would have even less than was normally prescribed. Using a nasal spray meant the drug would be absorbed more quickly into the bloodstream. If anything did go wrong, they could give Lisa an antidote to reverse the effects. As far as I was concerned, if it could relieve my daughter of her distressing symptoms then I was willing to go ahead with it. The doctor explained that Lisa would need to remain on the drug permanently and, if it worked, she could go home.

I gave my consent for the doctor to go ahead and I requested that if Lisa were to go into cardiac arrest, they should not try to revive her. This was not a decision I had taken lightly by any means, but I felt that my daughter had suffered enough, bearing in mind the recent deterioration in her condition.

Returning to the treatment room, I sat beside Lisa's bed and took her hand in mine once more. It was the only thing I *could* do. Having to watch her go through this was really hard and I tried to comfort her as best I could. It really helped to know that our church was praying for the family. God knew exactly what we needed and He was there for us the entire time, whether I was praying or not.

As I sat with Lisa, I suddenly found myself looking into eternity. I could see how it stretches on and on, without beginning or end. Moments later, I was completely enveloped in the love of God. The purity of the divine took my breath away. Within my spirit, I knew that this was what heaven feels like. I knew where my daughter was going and who she was going to be with, and this was of immense comfort to me at a time when I needed it the most. Lisa's body was dying but her spirit had life eternal.

Lisa turned her head and looked up at me. I could see in her eyes that she had had enough. It was time to ask that question again. I gazed lovingly at my beautiful, brave child and I asked in sign language, 'Do you want to go to heaven and live with Jesus?'

Too tired to speak, Lisa simply nodded. 'Yes.'

A male staff nurse entered the room, followed by the nursing sister. The tranquillising drug had been carefully measured to ensure the right dosage was administered. I explained to Lisa what was about to happen, that this would help her breathe more easily, and she nodded in acceptance. The young man applied the nasal spray into Lisa's nostrils and we stood around the bed to see what would happen next. It seemed to be working. Lisa's respiration rate decreased into a normal pattern, her body became relaxed and she fell into a deep and restful sleep. Confident that all was well, the nursing staff vacated the room.

A short while later, I realised that Lisa was not fast asleep but heavily sedated. She seemed completely unaware of her surroundings. Suddenly, I was hit by the full impact of the situation. My daughter was faced with two alternatives; she could either remain conscious and struggle to breathe, or be so drugged that she was oblivious to everything. In spite of her physical limitations, Lisa always made the most of what she had and sought to participate in what was going on around her. There was no way that she would want to carry on with either scenario, of that I was certain. Just the thought of watching my beloved daughter exist in a semi-comatose state day after day was unbearable. In the past fifteen years of my daughter's life, I had felt like a bicycle tyre with a slow puncture. But each time I felt deflated, God would reinflate me and put me back on the road again. It was different this time; I couldn't be reinflated any more. I had come to the end of the road and I began to implode.

The door opened and a nurse said, 'There's a phone call for you.'

I walked to the nurse's station nearby and picked up the phone. I was relieved to hear the voice of Pastor Maggie from church. After a brief update, Maggie asked, 'What would you like us to pray for?' I was so grateful to be asked that question. Usually when a Christian hears that a person is sick, or in hospital, they pray for that person's healing and there's nothing wrong with that. But Lisa and I had had enough. My daughter had already told me that she wanted to go to heaven. In response to Maggie's question, I replied, 'I want Him to take her home.'

After Maggie had prayed a quick prayer over the phone, I returned to my daughter's bedside. I flopped into an armchair near Lisa and in desperate need of a break, I picked up the magazine I'd bought and began to flick through the pages in a vain attempt to shut everything out. In the end, I was reading the same paragraph over and over again. My escape tactic hadn't worked and I put the magazine down.

That afternoon Lisa began to make a strange rattling noise in the back of her throat, caused by an accumulation of saliva. I had heard someone talk about it before. I knew what this meant. Known as 'the death rattle', it was a strong indication that death was near.

The atmosphere in the room began to change, as if charged with electricity, and I could sense the presence of angels, 'ministering spirits'[13] sent by God to provide comfort, and escort my daughter to heaven. I was not afraid. A supernatural peace filled the room.

Lisa had been under the influence of the drug for about an hour when I noticed something peculiar. She was repeatedly lifting her right shoulder from the pillow and then banging it down again. Straightaway I knew that Lisa was trying to attract my attention. Unable to open her eyes or speak, the only part of her body she seemed able to move was her right shoulder.

I called for help and the nursing sister arrived with the male nurse who had administered the tranquilliser. He walked to the far side of Lisa's bed, with the sister on the opposite side next to me. Not wanting to get in the way, I moved to the end of the bed. The sister took one look at my daughter and had the doctor paged. Lisa was in distress and a surge of panic rose within me. In that moment, in spite of everything I had previously felt or thought, I remembered the doctor telling me that if anything should go wrong they could give Lisa an antidote to reverse the effects of the drug. Without hesitation I instructed the nurse, 'Give her the antidote!'

The nurse looked at the sister and said, 'DNR.'

---

13. Hebrews 1:14, NKJV.

The doctor had written *Do Not Resuscitate* in Lisa's notes.

The nurse turned towards me, slowly shook his head and replied, 'No.'

The doctor arrived within minutes. We stood around the bed in silence and watched my daughter's life begin to slip away. No one intervened. Lisa's SATs were dropping steadily. 90-89-87 and down to 60. The numbers were red and they continued to fall. 54-53-52. When the number reached 45 the doctor placed his stethoscope on Lisa's chest to see if there was a heartbeat.

'It's very faint now.'

His voice was quiet.

The nurse wiped a tear from his cheek and walked slowly to the door without saying a word. As he passed by the sister, she lightly placed her arm on his and said, 'It's always difficult when it's a child.'

The sister switched off the SATs monitor. The IV catheter was removed from the back of Lisa's hand and the tube left dangling beside the bed. Saline solution fell onto the floor.

Drip ... drip ... drip ...

CHAPTER THIRTY-SEVEN

Saying Goodbye

My child was finally at peace. The doctor asked if I would like some time alone with my daughter, and I said, 'Yes.' He wrapped Lisa in her favourite woollen blanket of multicoloured patchwork squares, and carefully lifted her off the bed. As he did so, Lisa groaned. I would have found that very unnerving, except a few months previously a paramedic had told me that sometimes when a recently deceased person is moved, air trapped in the lungs is expelled, hence the groaning sound.

The doctor lowered my daughter onto my lap and then quietly left the room. Although she was fifteen years old, Lisa was the height of a ten-year-old and could easily fit onto my lap. I placed my arms around my daughter and I drew her against my chest in a warm embrace.

How could I ever let go?

The presence of God was thick in the room. Her head nestled into the crook of my arm, I gazed upon that sweet angelic face, still incredibly beautiful, even in death.

Hoping I wouldn't miss anything out, I told Lisa how much I loved her. I asked her to forgive me for not being a better mother. I said that I was sorry that her daddy had left us when she was only five years old. I said, 'I love you' again, just to make sure that she knew. I said, 'Thank you for being my daughter. Thank you for touching my heart and changing our lives in amazing ways.' I was confident that Lisa could still hear me. I spoke to her for a long time to be certain that I didn't leave anything out. After all, I would never be able to hold her in my arms again. Not in this lifetime, anyway.

Having said everything I needed to say, I paused for a few moments. The time had come to let her go. I whispered, 'Goodnight, Lisa, see you in the morning,' as I placed a gentle kiss upon her forehead. I was able to let her go in the knowledge that one day we would be together again. No more goodbyes.

Everything around me was still and serene. There was not a hint of pain or anguish.

'You can take her home now, Jesus.' I imagined Lisa's spirit surrounded by angels, escorting her to heaven.

The doctor returned and asked if I wanted Lisa to be put on the bed. I nodded.

When the doctor picked Lisa up, one of her arms fell limp beside her. It was dark purple in colour. The sight of that would have shocked me, had I not already been informed that when the heart stops beating the blood pools in the lower limbs, hence the discolouration to the skin. Lisa had also emptied her bladder, which is a common occurrence just after death because the muscles start to relax.

The nursing sister returned to the room and informed me that she would wash Lisa and arrange for her soiled clothes, her favourite orange pyjamas, to go to the laundry. I asked the sister if she had a nice white gown to put on Lisa because I wanted her to be clothed in something pretty, instead of a plain old hospital gown.

A few months previously, I had asked God for three things to happen when it was time for Lisa to die. I wanted it to happen in the London hospital. I wanted to be with her. And I wanted it to be peaceful. God had answered all three.

I left the room and did not look back.

A nurse led me into a side room so I could be alone for a while. I was grateful for the seclusion. Minutes later thoughts began swirling through my mind.

Is Lisa *really* dead?

What if her heart is still beating faintly?

What if the drugs have subdued her heartbeat but she's not really dead?

What if she revives in the mortuary and nobody knows about it?

I wanted the doctor to go back and check. And then double-check just to be certain.

The nurse had said that I could use the telephone in the room to make a few calls. I was now faced with the daunting task of informing Lisa's father that our daughter had just died. It was difficult to contact him, but when he returned my call an hour later and I broke the news to him, he was silent for a moment or two and then asked why I hadn't phoned earlier to let him know Lisa was in hospital. He sounded angry and upset. But I had seen no reason to contact him when Lisa was admitted the day before – I didn't know she was going to deteriorate so fast.

I realised that I had no way of getting home so I called Pastor Andrew and asked if he could arrange for someone to collect me from the hospital. He said he would fetch me himself, but it might take a while because he had some work to do first, and would probably get stuck in the rush hour traffic though London. I didn't mind having to wait. I could spend some time on my own to rest and gather my thoughts.

A nurse came in with a cup of tea. The staff Christmas party had been held in the room the previous day and she handed me some leftover food, three French loaves. It felt strange to be given some bread just after my daughter had died.

It was ten days before Christmas. The large silver and gold star in the treatment room seemed special to me and a nurse allowed me to take it home. 'Lisa's Star' would take pride of place amongst the festive decorations for years to come.

Lisa was examined by a doctor and a medical certificate issued, citing the cause of death as hypoventilation, plus axonal neuropathy. There it was in black and white. Yet, I still couldn't be convinced that Lisa was dead.

What if she was breathing just a little bit and no one noticed?

What if her heartbeat was really faint?

What if, what if, what if . . .

I had watched my daughter's blood oxygen levels gradually decrease from 90 down to 45 on the SATs monitor, but I did not see the number go down to 0. The seeds of doubt had been sown. My heart refused to accept what my brain already knew.

After a three-hour wait, Pastor Andrew arrived. He was kind and compassionate and it was just what I needed for the journey home. We reached the hospital's main entrance and stepped outside. It was cold. All of a sudden it dawned on me that I wasn't pushing a wheelchair any more. I felt a heavy weight lift off my shoulders, followed by a great sense of relief.

Jamie and Luke were waiting at home, but they were expecting me and Lisa. Throughout the journey, I tried to think of ways to tell my sons that their sister had died. Pastor Jerry had kindly offered to sit with the boys while I broke the news to them.

It was early evening when I arrived home. The lounge door was closed. Taking a deep breath, I opened the door and walked inside. Jerry was seated on one sofa, adjacent to Jamie and Luke, who were sat on the other.

'Hi, Mum!'

The boys leapt to their feet, ran over and threw their arms around me and I gave them a big hug. I was exhausted

physically and emotionally and I needed to sit down before I
fell down. I asked the boys to sit down beside me.

There was a silent pause.

Then Jamie looked towards the door and asked, 'Where's
Lisa?'

CHAPTER THIRTY-EIGHT

Telling the Children

Jamie's question echoed through the emptiness in my soul. How should I respond to a ten-year-old? Jamie needed to know and I didn't want to hurt him, but it *would* hurt him. All I could do was tell the truth as gently as I could.

'Lisa's gone home to heaven.'

'Is she dead?' said Luke.

For the next few seconds, Jamie, who absolutely adored his sister, sat in stunned silence and then burst into tears. He sobbed so hard I thought his heart would break. My soul twisted into a tight knot. Luke was wide-eyed with shock and didn't speak. When Jamie's tears had subsided, he turned to me and said, 'I'm upset because I never had the chance to say goodbye to Lisa.'

Pastor Jerry prayed for our family and then returned home. I turned to Jamie and suggested, 'Why don't you write a letter to Lisa and say what you want to say, then read it out to Jesus and ask Him to pass it on to her?' This seemed to comfort him and he settled down a bit.

'I'm going to draw a picture!' exclaimed Luke, and darted upstairs. My young son possessed a unique creative talent, not to mention a vivid imagination, and he expressed himself through drawing.

When Luke returned, he showed us his drawing of angels going up and down a stairway, with an open door at the top.

Jesus and Lisa stood side by side in the doorway, both of them smiling. Lisa was waving goodbye before she stepped through the door into heaven. 'She doesn't need her wheelchair any more!' Luke said. He seemed pleased about that.

The French loaves came in handy for the boys' supper, and I was grateful I didn't have to cook anything. We chatted for a while and it was soon bedtime. When they were tucked up in their beds, I gave the boys a big hug and told them I loved them.

I closed the lounge door behind me and I was alone. A tidal wave of grief came out of nowhere and swept over me. It was overwhelming. Gripped with panic, I thought, 'I can't do this!' Without hesitation, I rushed to the phone and dialled Pastor Jerry's number. Sandy, his wife, answered. I was too distraught to even speak, yet she somehow knew that it was me and said, 'I'll be right there!'

The moment Sandy walked into the lounge I fell into her arms and broke into a million pieces. My daughter was dead! Sandy was crying too. It was the first time that someone had actually wept with me. Strange as it may seem, it was comforting to know that I wasn't alone in my grief. Sandy stayed a while and then returned to her family.

In desperate need of sleep, I slowly made my way upstairs while holding onto the banister for support. Lisa's bedroom door was wide open. Just the sight of the hospital bed and her favourite Winnie the Pooh duvet cover was heart-breaking, and I had to close the door. As I lay in my bed, the day's events played over and over in my mind and I couldn't get to sleep. Finally, exhaustion took over and I drifted off.

When I awoke the next morning, my first thought was: 'It's time to get up and get Lisa ready for school.' But I didn't need to do that any more. I didn't panic. I felt nothing at all. The boys asked if they could have the day off school, and spent the day at home with me.

Jonathan made arrangements to visit the hospital mortuary viewing room to say goodbye to Lisa. When Jamie heard that his father was going that afternoon, he wanted to go too. I wasn't sure if Jamie could cope with seeing Lisa in that setting, but Jonathan assured me that he would take good care of him.

When he returned home, Jamie seemed calm and told me all about it.

'The room was nice; it had dimmed lights. Lisa was lying on a bed on the other side of a glass panel.' Seeing his sister one more time helped Jamie to say goodbye in his own way.

A few days later Jamie wrote a letter to his sister, and read it out to me. He and Lisa used to have lots of fun playing the card game 'Snap'. In the letter, he also talked about the fact that Lisa would poke out her tongue to people she liked. 'Are you having fun playing Snap with the crocodiles? And I can see you poking your tongue out at Jesus and making Him laugh!'

CHAPTER THIRTY-NINE

The Chapel of Rest

The selection of cards scattered across my front doormat each morning ranged between *Merry Christmas and a Happy New Year* to *Deepest Sympathy* and *Thinking of You*. Christmas Day was just around the corner. Life seemed to carry on as usual for everyone else. Supermarkets were filled with the hustle and bustle of people buying food for Christmas dinner, families and friends wondered what presents to buy their loved ones, and stores were crammed with shoppers going up one aisle and down the other trying to find the right gift. All the while, I had a funeral to arrange. Inside I was numb, but day after day felt carried along by an invisible wave. People were praying for my family and I was grateful.

Lisa's funeral could not take place without a death certificate. It was suggested that to save time, it would be better to formerly register Lisa's death in London because she had died in that area. Jonathan came with me. To my surprise, I was informed that a postmortem examination had not been carried out. Lisa's father was relieved, remarking that she had been through quite enough already.

An appointment was made with a funeral director in my home town. Pastor Maggie offered to come with me and I was grateful for her support; she was rarely lost for words and I could let her do most of the talking. The man behind the desk had a kind manner and gentle voice. He informed us that because Lisa had died in hospital and not at home there would be no need for an inquest, which might otherwise cause delays when arranging a funeral. Lisa's body could now be collected from the London hospital. After the body had been embalmed, Lisa would be prepared for viewing and placed in the Chapel of Rest for a few days. He said we could have the funeral before 25 December. I asked him if they had any coffins for children, to which he replied, 'Some new coffins came in this morning. There's one I think you might like.' He smiled, and continued, 'It's white, with silver handles in the shape of seashells.' My daughter loved playing on the beach and collecting seashells to take home. It was a very special coffin for a very special girl.

I had never been inside a Chapel of Rest before so I didn't know what to expect, but I did want to see Lisa one last time. One of my friends stayed at home with Jamie and Luke. They wanted to see their sister too, and if she looked OK then I would take the boys the following day. The Chapel of Rest was separate from the main building. I stood outside and tentatively put my hand on the doorknob. How would I react when I saw my daughter lying in a coffin? Steeling myself in anticipation, I turned the knob and stepped inside.

The room was sparsely furnished, and the décor was old-fashioned. The curtains were drawn and the lights dimmed, a faint glow illuminating the room. It was very cold.

On the far side of the room was a white coffin. The lid was open, revealing an interior of padded white satin.

Taking a deep breath, I walked over to the coffin and looked inside.

Lisa was clothed in a bridesmaid's dress she had worn for a friend's wedding. Made of cream fabric covered with pale pink and lilac flowers, I wanted her to look pretty when people came to see her. Lisa's beautiful shoulder-length chestnut brown hair, once so vibrant and shiny, now appeared dull, dry and lifeless. My heart sank. What had happened to her natural copper and gold highlights? Thankfully the bridesmaid's headdress, adorned with material flowers in cream and pink, helped to soften the blow a little.

My daughter lay totally still, her face calm and at rest. She looked like she was sleeping, except her eyelids had been glued shut. Some make-up had been applied to her face: a light foundation, blusher and pale pink lipstick to make her lips appear natural. My daughter had never worn make-up before, so it was quite an odd sight.

Lisa's arms were crossed over her chest. Her fingernails were dark blue. I wished someone had painted them.

Some rosary beads had been placed upon Lisa's hands, which I assumed were from Jonathan, given that his family were devout Catholics.

Seeing my daughter with straight legs was a big surprise. How was that possible? I wondered. Lisa's hips and knees had remained bent for years due to her shortened muscles.

As I stood on my own in the dimly lit room with my daughter in a coffin, a blanket of deep sadness came over me. I was too exhausted to weep. All those years of caring for a disabled child were at an end. I wouldn't be seeing her emaciated body any more.

Leaning forward, I placed a goodbye kiss on Lisa's forehead. Her skin was so cold.

That moment I realised, beyond all doubt, that my daughter was, in fact, dead. It was the final proof I needed.

Upon returning home, I walked into the kitchen to find my friend telling jokes with a neighbour and laughing, obviously hoping to lighten the atmosphere for me. But I couldn't take it. I had to get out of there, and fast. I turned around, and darted to my next-door neighbour's house. Abbey would know what to do.

When Abbey opened her front door all I could manage to say was, 'Have you got anything strong to drink?'

She invited me into her lounge and I sank into the armchair. I must have looked on the verge of collapse because Abbey went straight to her drinks' cabinet, no questions asked. All of a sudden I was hit by the reality of what I had just been through. My heart was gripped with panic and I was on the brink of losing control.

'What's wrong?' Abbey asked, as she handed me a large brandy.

'I've just seen Lisa in a coffin.'

I was trembling from head to foot.

CHAPTER FORTY

The Funeral

People wore bright colours to Lisa's funeral. She would have liked that. Our church organised a special Thanksgiving Service to commemorate my daughter's life, and all I had to do was be there on the day and hope that I didn't turn into a blubbering wreck.

A photo collage of Lisa was displayed in the entrance hall of the church. Some photos revealed Lisa's cheeky sense of humour, including one of her at the age of eight sat on my kitchen worktop swigging from an empty bottle of wine. In almost every photo Lisa was smiling. She smiled *a lot*!

The hall was packed and I was surprised to see so many people, including many I hadn't seen for a very long time. Someone had done a remarkable job tracking down Lisa's teachers and class assistants from years ago. It was heart-warming to think that my daughter had touched so many lives and they wanted to be part of her special day.

I made my way to the front row, greeting people along the way, and I took a seat beside Jamie and Luke. I wished I could hug my boys on the inside and make them feel better, but they seemed to be keeping it all together and I was grateful for the extra support from our church family.

Jonathan was sitting on the front row beside his wife on the opposite side of the hall. I felt a little aggrieved that he had not supported me through the difficult years but yet was here now, when it was too late. My father sat nearby with his wife, not far from my brother and his family, and I was grateful for their support.

After singing a couple of well-chosen songs, Jonathan went to the front and addressed the crowd. He thanked everyone for coming and said a few words about his daughter.

Then Mr Jones, the headteacher of the school for the deaf, made his way forward. It was such a pleasant surprise to have him with us that day. He spoke very kindly about Lisa and shared a comical story about her antics at school. He told about how one day she hadn't been seen downstairs for a while and a member of staff went to her bedroom to see if she was OK. Knocking hard on the door, they waited for a response, but none came. For some reason the door wouldn't open. Knocking again, they called out, 'Lisa, are you OK? Can you open the door?' Still no response.

After repeated attempts to gain entry, it was thought that Lisa might be jammed against the door. As time passed, they became more and more concerned. Maybe she was in a life-threatening situation? The staff began to fear that something untoward must have happened. Maybe Lisa couldn't respond because she was unconscious? They *had* to do something, but how could they get in?

The local fire brigade was busy on another call. The school's groundsman had locked the ladder in a shed and taken the key home. The only way to reach Lisa was through the first-floor window, and the only way to reach that was to shimmy up the drainpipe. Mr Jones volunteered because he wouldn't let his staff take the risk.

Ripples of laughter echoed around the hall as Mr Jones recounted how he clambered up the wall, holding the drainpipe, and prayed the brackets would hold firm. When he had reached the same level as the window, he carefully sidled along a narrow ledge. The sash window was closed but not locked. Mr Jones peered through the glass and spotted Lisa straightaway. Mystery solved. The staff couldn't open the bedroom door because Lisa had rammed her electric wheelchair against it to prevent anyone from getting in and was sitting there laughing!

Mr Jones climbed through the window and came face-to-face with the culprit. I'm sure Lisa was surprised to see him standing there, because she wouldn't have expected anyone to come through the window! Informing his staff that Lisa was all right, Mr Jones steered the wheelchair away from the door and told Lisa, kindly but firmly, never to do that again.

None of us had heard the story before, not even me, and I was grateful to Mr Jones for injecting some light relief into the service. Lisa seemed to have left an imprint on people's hearts wherever she went.

Soon it was my turn to speak. I stepped onto the platform and steeled myself to read a poem. A strong wave of fatigue caught me unawares and I had to grab hold of the lectern to stop myself from falling over. In need of support, I turned to Pastor Andrew, who was sitting behind me, and motioned for him to come alongside me. I took a deep breath, then began to read the poem I had written:

No more hospitals, no more tears,
no more pain, and no more fears.
Resurrection, and release,
Look to heaven, receive His peace.

At the end of the service, adults I hadn't seen for many years offered their condolences.

Some might find it odd that we had a Thanksgiving Service, but it was our way of acknowledging that Lisa had been a blessing to many.

After the service, family and friends made their way to the local cemetery for a traditional funeral service held in a small chapel. Lisa's burial was the one thing I dreaded most. My mother was waiting at the cemetery with her husband, Bill. She was clothed in black from head to foot.

Upon entering the small grey-stone chapel, my eyes were drawn to the white coffin at the front but my heart did not perceive what my eyes were seeing. The chapel was almost full and I was the last person to arrive. I could barely put one foot in front of the other as I made my way to the front row and sat beside Jamie and Luke on the wooden pew. My boys were so brave that day. My mother and her husband sat behind us, with my father and his wife across the aisle. Jonathan and his wife were near the back of the chapel.

I felt very alone.

I turned my attention to the polished white coffin with silver shell handles and the reality hit me.

Lisa, my daughter, was inside that coffin.

We were at her funeral.

I was still numb after her death. I felt disconnected from everything around me. I didn't cry. I had no tears left.

Pastor Andrew took his position at the front and shared a few words befitting the occasion, his tender-hearted nature a soothing balm to a grieving mother's heart.

The service drew to a close. It was time to put Lisa in the ground. Everyone was waiting for me to stand to my feet and lead them out, but I could not move. My legs had seized up and I was glued to the spot. I tried to attract Andrew's attention, but I couldn't speak.

Praying a silent 'help' to God, my legs started to work again and I rose to my feet. Lisa's coffin went out first and I walked behind with the boys. The coffin was placed in a hearse and we followed in a shiny black car. It was a freezing cold day in December. Snowflakes fell from a grey sky and kissed the earth.

A row of flowers and wreaths lined the way, declaring comfort and love. Our friends had chosen to walk ahead of us, and Pastor Maggie, wearing high heels, as she always did, slid on the icy ground, arms and legs going in all directions in an attempt to maintain her balance. Lisa would have found that really funny!

We gathered around the coffin and I placed my arms around my sons and drew them close.

Taking a few steps forward, I placed a single red rose on top of the pristine white coffin.

My mother leaned forward and placed an envelope upon the coffin. Inside the envelope was a letter to Lisa written by my sister.

Lisa's coffin was lowered into the grave. Someone asked me if I wanted to throw some dirt into the grave and I said, 'No.' It seemed an odd custom to me. Some did take a handful of dirt and throw it onto the casket; maybe it was their way of paying their last respects. Pastor Maggie reached into her coat pocket, then scattered multicoloured rose petals into the grave, which floated gently down and settled upon Lisa's coffin. That really blessed me.

Then the funeral was over and people began to leave.

I remained for a while.

After some moments on my own, I turned and walked away to the sound of men shovelling earth into Lisa's grave.

CHAPTER FORTY-ONE

Christmas Without Lisa

Christmas was just days away and the cards kept coming: beautiful pictures of snow-covered landscapes, Santa with his red-nosed reindeer, and Christmas stockings dangling above a roaring fireplace beside a bedecked Christmas tree. Opening the cards, they read:

To Ana, Lisa, Jamie and Luke
A Merry Christmas and a Happy New Year

But Lisa wasn't here! Each time I read my daughter's name it hurt. News of Lisa's death hadn't reached everyone yet. The majority of Christmas cards wished us a 'Happy New Year'. How on earth was next year supposed to be *happy*? The cards did provide an extra splash of colour to the lounge. 'Lisa's Star' took pride of place amidst the Christmas decorations, the silver and gold star a reminder of heaven touching earth in the London hospital.

Seven days after Lisa died it was her brother's eighth birthday. I tried to make the day as cheery as I could for Luke's sake, but a very special person was missing and it affected us all.

Facing Christmas without a loved one, especially for the first time, can be a daunting experience. How could I possibly get excited about the festivities when I had just buried my daughter? All I wanted to do was hide under the duvet and stay there until it was all over. But I had my boys to consider, so I put on a brave face. Someone must have injected some lignocaine into my soul because I didn't feel a thing.

Lisa's presents had already been wrapped and were under the Christmas tree amongst the other gifts. Each time I laid eyes on her presents it was a reminder, *she's not here, she's dead*. Would this pain ever go away?

Unable to part with Lisa's gifts, I put them all in her bedroom and kept the door closed until I was ready to decide what to do with them.

Christmas Day came and went. It was all a blur. I was physically present but emotionally absent. At one point, Jamie suddenly burst out laughing, but stopped himself mid-flow because he felt guilty.

'Mum, do you think it's wrong for me to laugh?' said Jamie.

'No, love,' I replied, tenderly. 'Lisa often made us laugh.'

For a while, each morning when I awoke my first thought was to take Lisa to the toilet, and it took a while to reprogramme my brain. The realisation 'she's not here' pricked like a thorn. Lisa's bedroom door was kept shut because I couldn't bear the sight of the hospital bed and medical equipment.

The day would come when I'd have to sort through Lisa's belongings. Taking anything out of her room meant 'she's gone and she's not coming back' and the finality was difficult to bear. If I threw anything away, wasn't that the same as throwing Lisa away? It might seem irrational, but that's how I felt. A bereaved parent might leave a child's bedroom untouched for months, even years, before they decide what to do with the room. Family members or friends need to be patient and not try to coax them into doing something they're not ready for.

Every now and then I heard Lisa's voice call out to me at home. It was the sound she used to make to attract my attention when she needed something. Apparently, this phenomenon is referred to as 'ghosting' and can be part of the grieving process. This occurred over a short period of time and I never heard it again.

My daughter had gone from 'present tense' to 'past tense'. I was afraid of forgetting what she looked like, and how she sounded when she was singing.

A few weeks after Lisa was buried, I paid my first visit to her grave. The earth had sunk a few inches and the sight of it disturbed me. At the head of the grave was a simple wooden cross to indicate who was buried there. I wanted Lisa to have a proper gravestone but couldn't afford one. The colourful wreaths and flowers placed upon the grave at Lisa's funeral were now faded and discoloured. I picked up the withered remains and threw them in the bin.

For the first four months after Lisa died I felt carried along by a wave that was both gentle and strong. Occasionally someone from church brought my family a home-cooked meal and it was really appreciated. When we received a 'Thinking of You' card through the letterbox it meant a lot to me too. Often a few comforting words did far more good than verses of scripture telling me what I should be doing, or how I should be feeling, when all I wanted to do was curl up and die.

After the initial four-month period, visits, cards and phone calls became much less frequent. Our level of care dwindled from a flow to a trickle. My family were no longer in need of intensive care and people diverted their attention to more pressing issues. Thankfully, close friends were never far away.

My sons were hurting too and needed my attention, but I couldn't always give it to them. Sometimes I was too wrapped up in my own sorrow, or tried to ignore what I was feeling. When Lisa died, I received a lot of support from others, but Jamie and Luke needed someone to spend time with them too.

My sons expressed grief in different ways. Jamie, who was almost eleven, often came to me when he was worried or upset. He didn't mind showing his emotions in front of his mum. It's OK for boys to cry. We did shed a few tears together, but sometimes Jamie cried on his own because he didn't want to upset me. For a while after his sister died, Jamie wore a baseball cap everywhere he went with the peak pulled down. My eldest son had been through such a lot already and was growing up much too fast, an old head on young shoulders. At times, I felt Jamie wanted to take care of *me* instead of the other way round.

Jamie was very fortunate to have a class teacher who was also a qualified child bereavement counsellor. Knowing that she was keeping a special eye on Jamie was very comforting, and I couldn't help feeling that God had something to do with it.

Luke, who was usually full of energy, became withdrawn and didn't talk very much. He began to suffer from headaches. He was crying at school one day when his class teacher, who was known for being strict, sat Luke on her lap and gave him a hug.

It was apparent from Luke's drawings that he had suffered a major upheaval in his life. There were no more vibrant colours. He used a black felt pen and little else, except red. The illustrations took on a macabre theme of graveyards, gravestones and gore. People were stabbed and dying, blood oozing from their wounds or dripping from the assailant's knife. Luke was exploring the issues of death and dying through his graphic artwork.

Not long after Lisa died, Luke was beset by the fear of death. Now his sister had died, he couldn't help wondering who was next. He had always slept in the dark, but now he wanted the landing light to stay on all night and his bedroom door kept slightly open. I think he liked to hear me moving around downstairs and could only get to sleep if he knew I was close by.

Whenever my sons asked me questions about Lisa, I would always be honest with them and answer the best way I knew how, taking their ages into consideration. Luke wanted to know some of the details regarding what had happened to Lisa's body after she died, and as he was only eight years old, I had to choose my words very carefully. He wasn't sure how to deal with it all, and his friends were too young to offer the support he needed.

Years later, Luke told me that throughout his sister's life, he wasn't fully aware of what was going on, whereas adults close to the family seemed to know what was happening more than he did. I hadn't realised that Luke had felt that way, and wished I had taken the time to explain things to him while his sister was alive.

As the initial shock of Lisa's death began to wear off, it wasn't long before I was confronted by an identity crisis. Everything had been structured around caring for a child with special needs. Life had become easier in some ways, but more difficult in others. After fifteen years immersed in a carer's role, how could I remove the essence of who I had become? I didn't know who to 'be' without Lisa. What kind of person was I now? I was still a single mum with two sons to take care of, but they didn't demand the same time and attention as Lisa had. My loss of identity was a dark chasm which grew wider and wider as the days went by.

Lisa, my supernova, had shone brightly for a while and then she was gone. A future without her seemed unfathomable. My soul drifted around in its own personal space, with no stars to navigate by or satellites to communicate with.

Anaesthetised to life, I still went through the motions of day-to-day living: get up in the morning, give the boys breakfast, drift through the day like tumbleweed in the desert, make the boys supper and eventually go to bed. The next day was just the same, and the next and the next. I was glad that my boys were with me, because they kept me moving forward. Having some sort of daily routine meant I had to continue, regardless of the fact that I merely coasted through life on autopilot.

But the question remained: *If I wasn't a carer any more, then who was I?*

Not long after that, I attended a weekend for bereaved parents. It was just what I was looking for. At last I could talk to people who understood first-hand what I was going through and could help on my journey to recovery. Spending time with other parents who had suffered the loss of a child meant a safe environment where we could unpack our feelings and receive hope for the future.

On the last evening of the weekend, I felt God wanted me to get up early in the morning and watch the sunrise.

It was still dark outside. I pulled my coat around me to guard against the cold night air.

The sky was pitch black. Stars twinkled in space. It was so dark I could barely see the landscape. All around was quiet. Nothing moved. At first, I could barely see and had to squint to get a better look. In the far distance, a faint rose-pink glow appeared on the horizon as darkness gave way to light. Paintbrush in hand, the Creator of the universe mixed shades of pink on His artist's palette and adorned the firmament with colours that became deeper, richer and more glorious with each passing moment. A rose-coloured mantle had settled upon the earth.

A sweet melody of birdsong wafted through the air to praise the new day. There's something about that sound; it's like medicine to the soul.

Where the earth met the sky, the tip of a golden globe began its grand entrance and continued ascending until its full glory was revealed. The sun took centre stage. Creation was bid 'arise and shine'[14] and the landscape was now bathed in golden hues. From amongst the hedgerows and out of burrows, furry inhabitants awakened from their slumber and a rabbit hopped across the meadow in search of food.

The invitation to witness the sunrise had not been in vain.

For the first time in a very long while, I had hope for the future.

Having been through the long 'dark night of the soul', I was now embarking on a brand-new chapter.

---

14. See Isaiah 60:1.

CHAPTER FORTY-TWO

Birthday Balloons

How could we possibly celebrate Lisa's birthday when she was no longer with us? She would have been sixteen. It was a bittersweet day. After a trip into town to buy a bunch of flowers and three helium balloons with 'Happy Birthday' emblazoned across them in bright colours – one from me, one from Jamie and the other from Luke – my sons and I headed off to the cemetery.

The ground was covered by a layer of frost and glistened in the sunlight like a carpet of diamonds. Standing at the foot of the grave alongside Lisa's brothers, I placed my arms around my boys and drew them closer. Having almost resigned myself to the fact that Lisa had gone, the pain in my heart was not as acute as in previous months, but visiting the grave was still hard to do. I thought momentarily, 'What must it be like for her, buried way down in the cold earth?' But of course I knew that she couldn't feel it because she wasn't there. Lisa was in a much better place where the light always shone and sickness was no more.

I placed the flowers upon her grave, the multicoloured petals a stark contrast to the hardened winter soil.

The helium balloons swayed aloft in the breeze as we held onto the ribbons until it was time to let go.

A few lone adults tended to the graves of their loved ones. We must have looked an unusual sight as we stood in the graveyard holding 'Happy Birthday' balloons, but I didn't care what other people thought. We wanted to mark Lisa's special day in a personal way.

Saying, 'I love you,' we released our balloons. The helium caused them to float upwards, and they continued higher and higher as if guided by unseen hands. As I gazed at the balloons, I remembered that great and awful day when Lisa had breathed her last and her spirit went up to heaven.

My boys and I imagined the balloons reaching heaven and Lisa catching them. We wanted her to know that she wasn't forgotten and we still loved her very much. It comforted us to imagine that Lisa might be able to see us releasing the balloons. She loved receiving helium balloons on her birthday. I used to tie them to her hospital bed until they began to deflate and float down to the floor. I had given Lisa a helium balloon on her fifteenth birthday, just a month before she died. It had red roses and 'I love you' printed on it.

We looked up into the sky and kept our eyes on the balloons until we couldn't see them any more.

Then it was time to go home.

CHAPTER FORTY-THREE

The New Children's Hospice

During my daughter's life, the mere mention of the word 'hospice' filled me with fear and dread. Isn't that where people go to die? As far as I was concerned, a hospice meant only one thing – 'Your child is dying' – and I didn't want to accept that.

A couple of years after Lisa died, I was at home praying when an image came to mind of an architect's drawing of a new children's hospice with a central courtyard. Around that time, the image of an oak tree kept popping up in various places. I felt it was relevant but had no idea why. I was about to find out.

Spending all day at home with nothing to do, I soon became lonely and bored. Realising that I needed to get out and about, I decided to offer my services at a charity shop. A few days later I spotted the sign 'Volunteer Wanted' in the window of the local hospice shop and went inside to enquire about the position. The manageress, Susan, invited me into the office for an interview there and then.

The position involved sorting through bags of donated clothes to separate unsaleable items from those in good condition, and displaying garments on the shop floor. After the interview, I was offered the job and accepted. Susan and I continued to chat over a cup of tea.

'Have you heard about the new children's hospice they want to build, next to the adult hospice?'

'No, I haven't,' I replied, intrigued.

'I don't know much about it, except they want to build it next to an oak tree.'

The moment she said the words 'oak tree', I knew. It made sense of the oak trees I kept seeing, and the image of the architect's plan sprang to mind.

A few days later my attention was drawn to a local newspaper article about plans for a new children's hospice in the neighbouring town. A member of hospice staff invited parents with past experience of raising a child with a life-limiting condition to contact them if they were interested in being involved in the project. After a brief phone call to the hospice, I was invited to attend an informal gathering the following day.

As I drove up the narrow road leading to The Pasque Adult Hospice (Luton and South Bedfordshire Hospice prior to 1998) on the outskirts of Luton, I had mixed feelings. I was about to enter a building I had spent so long trying to avoid!

After parking the car, I steeled myself for what lurked within, made my way towards the main entrance and stepped tentatively inside. The modern reception area was infused with light, a far cry from the dark and gloomy interior I had imagined. Neutral tones complimented the exposed wood, and bunches of flowers added to the calm, soothing ambience. I was surprised and felt at ease straightaway. There wasn't even a hint of the awful smell of disinfectant that seemed to go hand-in-hand with hospitals.

The receptionist asked me to take a seat while she informed a member of staff of my arrival. Moments later a woman walked past me carrying a tea tray – pristine white china upon a white linen cloth with embroidered edges, and a small vase containing a delicate sprig of flowers. She smiled as she went by. It seemed more like a five-star hotel than a hospice.

The matron offered me a warm welcome and led me down a corridor, chatting along the way. We went into a side room where approximately thirty adults were engaged in conversation. Men and women had come to offer their time and expertise towards developing the new children's hospice, including nurses, a physiotherapist and a pharmacist. Matron was joined at the front of the room by hospice staff members, including the current nursing manager.

Matron informed us of plans to raise 3 million pounds to build a new children's hospice on land adjoining the adult facility. It would offer a palliative care service to families across two counties where, according to research, an estimated 300 children had been diagnosed as having a life-limiting condition. A holistic model of health care would attend to families' physical, psychological, social and spiritual needs. The children's hospice would provide a safe environment where children could play and make new friends while receiving medical treatment. Parents would be able to leave their child at the hospice while they took a well-earned break. The child's siblings would also be cared for. Support would be available to families through bereavement and beyond. These services would be offered free of charge.

How I wished such a place had existed to help my family during our time of need.

The attendees were instructed to form small groups to get to know one another better, and each group would then nominate a person whom they felt would be a valuable asset to the team. A buzz filled the room, the conversation interrupted ten minutes later by the matron declaring, 'We need a PR person!' Without hesitation, a member of my group, a Justice of the Peace from the local Magistrates' Court, looked me straight in the eye and announced, 'That's you, Ana!' I was quite taken aback; we had only just met and she barely knew me. My name was put forward and I was elected to join the planning and building team for the new children's hospice as a spokesperson for families in need of their services.

The planning and building team, overseen by the hospice general manager consisted of highly qualified personnel with a knowledge of palliative care that was far beyond my personal experience. Nevertheless, we had a mutual respect for one another and were united in our goal. This proved a solid foundation on which to build. My fellow team members also took into account that I had personal experience of raising a child with a life-limiting condition and were very supportive. I knew what a huge difference it would make to others, and therefore poured my heart and soul into the project.

In April 1998 the children's hospice appeal was launched and we got off to a flying start when a local businessman donated £1 million – £500,000 at the launch of the project, and the remaining amount to be matched pound-for-pound up to the first £500,000 received in other donations. After discussions amongst hospice management and trustees, it was decided that the new children's hospice be named in honour of our generous benefactor and therefore became Keech Cottage Children's Hospice. The new logo depicted a blue house with a white heart. Fund-raising continued and the children's hospice began to take shape.

Another aspect of campaigning for a new children's hospice was to spread the word across the region to other health care professionals and Social Services regarding the specialist services that would be offered to families. By forming a network, parents could be informed about the children's hospice shortly after their child was initially diagnosed. Bearing in mind there were already skilled professionals working in the field of palliative care in the region, and doing a sterling job too, the new children's hospice could support even more families in need.

A public speaking training course was held for volunteers at the hospice. I was eager to utilise my newly acquired skills, and nervous too. A series of public speaking engagements ensued, accompanied by the hospice appeals manager. We spoke in various establishments across the county, including schools and colleges, community groups and churches. Roger explained the services to be provided by the new children's hospice and the funds needed to build and maintain the facility, with running costs for the first year estimated at £900,000. After Roger's presentation, I then shared my personal account of family life without a hospice, and the difference it would make if families had someone to turn to.

Before each speaking engagement, I made enquiries about the particular group I was addressing, and then formulated an appropriate theme as an ice breaker to help put the audience at ease. Preferring to speak from the heart rather than use notes, I incorporated a couple of humorous anecdotes to ensure the message wasn't too heavy. Sickness, death and bereavement is an emotive subject. On occasion, some members of the audience shed a few tears, particularly those who had recently suffered a personal loss. In my experience, a few carefully chosen words helped to quash people's fear of the unknown. After my talk, people sometimes approached me and shared their story and I was able to comfort them.

My public relations and fund-raising role also led me into the world of advertising and marketing, and I discovered a river of creativity deep within me that I didn't know was there. My mind was popping with straplines and ideas for the design and layout of posters and leaflets to advertise the new children's hospice. I was by no means a key player in that particular department, but the opportunity to submit my ideas and then see them in print was very rewarding.

When a member of staff requested some photographs of Lisa to include in their material, I was faced with a dilemma. The only professional photographs I had of Lisa were taken when she was a toddler. I wished I had arranged more when she was older. Only a small number of photographs, taken with a disposable camera, were of sufficient quality to enlarge and print.

It was strange to see my daughter's face emblazoned across the front of A4-sized posters and leaflets. One of the photos showed Lisa drawing a picture. She had a big smile on her face and her thin forearms were covered in felt-pen ink. Above Lisa's photo was the caption, 'Help Us to Help Others'.

Another steep learning curve was engaging with the media – press, television and radio – and I soon learned how important it was to choose my words very carefully. Once something is said it cannot be taken back again. In spite of my best efforts, I was misquoted by the press on at least one occasion. When a newspaper reporter enquired about the day Lisa died, I explained to her that due to a shortage of hospital beds Lisa was placed in the treatment room, which at the time was also being used as a storeroom. When the article was printed, I was shocked to discover that it stated my daughter had died in a room not much bigger than a broom cupboard!

The local radio station BBC's Three Counties Radio requested an interview to promote the children's hospice, and arrangements were made for me to visit their premises and tell my story.

Sometime later, a film crew from Anglia TV's regional news programme was at the hospice to record a segment with a senior member of staff. Then it was my turn to be interviewed. Instead of filming on-site, they had a sudden change of plan and said they would rather film me at home – right then! After the initial shock, and a very quick tidy-up of my home, the film crew arrived and did the interview.

The children's hospice appeal was aired on Anglia TV the following week. The segment began with the reporter speaking to staff at the hospice. Then a photograph of Lisa wearing her bridesmaid's dress filled the screen. It was surreal and it seemed very odd. I wanted to press the 'pause, rewind' button and bring Lisa back to life. I didn't want my daughter to be dead. I wanted her here with me.

It was odd to watch myself on television and I tried to get my head around the fact that Lisa had just been seen, and our story heard, by millions of people. Even now, my precious daughter was touching the hearts and minds of people across the east of England. Her life was still making a difference, not only to me but countless others too. Somehow, I had the feeling it was only a glimpse of a much bigger picture.

The children's hospice was opened on 28 March 2000 by HRH Princess Anne, who planted an oak tree in memory of Lisa outside the main entrance. (Incidentally, we also had a lovely chat about our children.)

During my voluntary work for the hospice, a member of staff discovered that I couldn't afford to buy a gravestone for Lisa. They organised a whip-round in the office and people dipped into their pockets to contribute towards the overall cost. Their kind and thoughtful gesture moved me to tears.

As instructed, I paid a visit to the local memorial mason to choose a gravestone and inscription. When I arrived, a kind gentleman informed me that the cost had already been covered. Mindful that someone else was paying for the gravestone, I chose something modest. I decided on a medium-sized heart, made of white marble, plus gold-engraved lettering. I requested that the stone be placed at the head of the grave at a slight angle off the ground. A hospice staff member requested the Keech Cottage logo be incorporated into the design, which I thought was entirely appropriate given my involvement with the team, their incredible support towards my family, and the ongoing work of the new children's hospice for years to come.

A couple of weeks later, I paid a visit to the cemetery to see the new memorial. I was in for a big surprise! Instead of the medium-sized gravestone laid at an angle upon the earth, stood a large heart-shaped memorial in pristine white marble. It took my breath away!

Around the perimeter of the grave was a white marble kerb and the centre was filled with vivid-blue shiny glass chippings. At the foot of the kerb, embossed into the marble, was a small blue house with a white heart. I knew that many hearts would find a home at Keech Cottage.

It was such a fitting memorial to an incredible young lady.

Stood at the foot of the grave, I was overcome by the generosity of the hospice staff and I started to cry.

Engraved in the headstone written in gold was Lisa's name, her date of birth and the date she died.

The inscription was compiled by myself, Jamie and Luke, and it encapsulated what we wanted the world to know about a special young lady who would always be loved, and who loved others unconditionally.

Much loved
Loved much
Jesus gave you the gift of a lifetime

1)24